The Official
Garlic Lovers
Handbook

Ode to Garlic

Sudden, it comes for you
in the cave of yourself where you know
and are lifted by important events.
Say you are dining and it happens:
soaring like an eagle, you are
pierced by the message from the midst of life.
Memory—what holds the days together—
touches
your tongue. It is from deep in the earth
and it reaches out kindly, saying, "Hello,
Old Friend."
It makes us all alike, all offspring of powerful
forces, part of one great embrace of
democracy,
united across every boundary.
You walk out generously, giving it back
in a graceful wave, what you've been
given.
Like a child again, you breathe on the
world, and it shines.

William Stafford
Poet Laureate of the State of Oregon

THE OFFICIAL
GARLIC
LOVERS
HANDBOOK

Lloyd John Harris
Lovers of the Stinking Rose
with a preface by Alice Waters

ARIS BOOKS
BERKELEY, CALIFORNIA

Library of Congress Cataloging in Publication Data

Harris, Lloyd J., 1947–
    The official garlic lovers handbook.

    Bibliography: p.
    1. Cookery (Garlic) 2. Garlic. I. Lovers of the
Stinking Rose (Group: Berkeley, Calif.) II. Title.
TX819.G3H37 1986 641.6′526 86-8007
ISBN 0–943186–15–3

Aris Books are published by
Harris Publishing Company, Inc.
1621 Fifth Street
Berkeley, CA 94710
(415) 527-5171

Book trade distribution by Simon and Schuster,
a division of Simon & Schuster, Inc.
Simon & Schuster Building
Rockefeller Center
1230 Avenue of the Americas
New York, NY 10020

Book design: Seventeenth Street Studios
Typesetting: Another Point, Inc.

Printed and bound in the United States of America
First Printing: May 1986

10 9 8 7 6 5 4 3 2

Disclaimer and Warning

Garlic is a potent food, loved and used throughout the world, and is considered non-toxic when used in reasonable amounts. However, with different constitutions, garlic can, like many foods, cause a variety of effects, from gas and nausea to euphoria and giddiness. Eaten raw, garlic can irritate the stomach lining and burn fingers and lips. Some people are allergic to garlic. They may or may not be vampires.

Excessive garlic usage can affect job security and social status, and although LSR is dedicated to erasing the stigma of garlic consumption, we would be less than candid if we didn't remind the reader that there is still stiff resistance to the Garlic Revolution.

Garlic has been used as an aphrodisiac in Asia and elsewhere, but LSR makes no claims. We have noted increased frivolity and an abandonment of inhibitions when garlic is consumed in vast quantitites (helping professions take note). At the same time, excessive garlic consumption can lead to a form of alcoholism, in that garlic increases the speed with which the blood-stream absorbs alcohol. So, although you may choose to drive after only one drink, don't drive after one drink plus Pesto.

Garlic has been associated with the devil and is considered taboo by certain religions, mostly Eastern in persuasion. We make no judgment in this regard. Medical research is pointing to garlic's uses in cardiovascular disorders, fungal and bacterial infectiohs, and other conditions, but again, we make no claims in this regard and caution all garlic lovers to consult their physician before self-treating with garlic. But, if your physician tries to persuade you against the use of garlic, talk to your local herbalist or acupuncturist or other alternative health practitioner.

Finally, *The Official Garlic Lovers Handbook* is intended for the serious garlic user. The garlic novice emerging from the closet (including the horizontal kind with lids, if you catch our drift) might do well to start with *The Book of Garlic* or any of the other fine garlic books on the market (see Garlic Bibliography).

Lovers of the Stinking Rose

Table of Contents

IV. Garlic: The Medicine

V. Garlic: A Miscellany

Preface

≈ ALICE WATERS ≈

IT WAS EXACTLY 10 years ago that Chez Panisse celebrated its first Bastille Day garlic "gala," and since then the restaurant has never been the same. Each summer, a kind of garlic frenzy overtakes the restaurant. (One year we printed "Garlic Frenzy" on the festival menu.) People have come from all over California to participate; food writers ask for interviews; and our reservations people are inundated, with little defense except to say, "We are sold out, but 50 other restaurants are now participating." Last year it was just too much, and, with Berkeley, Los Angeles, and Gilroy having festivals, I had to wonder what this garlic mania was all about.

When John Harris suggested that Chez Panisse start a garlic festival, I was charmed by the idea. John had been a waiter during our first few chaotic weeks in business, so he has a familiarity with the spirit of the restaurant. I had just been working on our July 14th Bastille Day menu, and the idea of making it a Garlic Festival worked especially well, because it coincided with the garlic harvest. My own passion for garlic had evolved during trips to France, and particularly from the remarkable profusion of garlic tastes in Provençe. Sharing my growing pleasure in garlic's strong but versatile nature with our customers was perfectly achieved through the festival. And what a wonderful time we had that year. Each year since 1976, the crowds grew, demanding more and more garlic! It wasn't enough to serve whole heads of roasted new garlic or grilled chicken smothered in garlic purée—we had to put it in the dessert!

I had a garlic-deprived childhood, which might explain the effect of those taste voyages to Provençe, and garlic was one of the catalysts that led to our kind of cooking at Chez Panisse. You cannot ignore garlic: you either *eat* garlic or you leave it alone. I think it was Les Blank (who shot much of his film, *Garlic Is as Good as Ten Mothers*, at the restaurant) who said after the first Garlic Festival, "There is no such thing as too much garlic." This contradicts the traditional American attitude to garlic that says, in effect, "There is no such thing as too *little* garlic." Garlic's direct quality wakes up the sense of taste, and this is what American food needs above all.

Of course there is more to garlic than its magic in the kitchen. There is a mystique about garlic because of its therapeutic properties and its folklore. The Lovers of the Stinking Rose and John have managed to digest all this garlic information in *The Book of Garlic*. But now, with *The Official Garlic Lovers Handbook*, this garlic obsession could affect an even broader audience.

What I think I appreciate most about the *Handbook* is that it explains how garlic can find its right use depending on its variety, the time of the year it is picked, and the kinds of foods with which it is served. All ingredients can be understood this way and *need* to be understood this way. Garlic is perhaps the first food that taught me this important lesson.

If *The Official Garlic Lovers Handbook* succeeds in its mission to launch garlic festivals all over America, perhaps some of the focus will be taken off of Chez Panisse's festival. Then we'll have our old-fashioned Garlic Gala again, with a little room to breathe!

Acknowledgments and Notes on Contributors

T*HE OFFICIAL* Garlic Lovers Handbook is essentially an anthology of writings and recipes. Although I have contributed some of the pieces and much of the connective tissue between pieces, I am extremely grateful to all the talented garlic lovers who have contributed material to this book. Many of them contributed to *The Book of Garlic* and over the years to the newsletter of Lovers of the Stinking Rose, *Garlic Times*.

Those who have kept the faith through thick and thin should be singled out. You have kept me going:

Sahag and Elizabeth Avedisian of the Cheese Board for their loyalty, vision, and humor.

Les Blank and Maureen Gosling for their film—*Garlic Is as Good as Ten Mothers*—correspondence, and photographs.

Charles Perry for his leadership in Los Angeles and endless craziness.

Alice Waters et al. at Chez Panisse for giving me my first heavy dose.

My family for sticking by me through it all.

Those contributing major sections to the book deserve special thanks and special note:

Lynda Brown is an anthropologist and a food and garden writer. Her book, *Fresh Thoughts on Food*, was published in 1986 (Chatto and Windus). She lives in North Yorkshire, Great Britain.

Susan Chamberlin is a landscape architect and horticultural writer living in Santa Barbara, California. She is the author of *Hedges, Screens & Espaliers* (HP Books).

Pat Darrow, formerly a member of two Berkeley food collectives, the Cheese Board and the Swallow Cafe, is currently writing fiction and poetry. Her cooking is an inspiration. She lives in Walnut Grove, California.

Alexandra H. Hicks is an internationally known food and herb consultant, researcher, garden designer, writer, and popular lecturer. She is a member of the Herb Society of America and the British Herb Society, and teaches at several universities. She lives in Ann Arbor, Michigan.

James Paul is a poet, journalist, and editor living in San Francisco, California. He was very involved in launching this project.

Charles Perry is the Southern California leader of Lovers of the Stinking Rose. He is also a restaurant reviewer for the *Los Angeles Times*, West Coast editor for *Cook's Magazine*, and a lecturer on food history. He lives in Sylmar, California.

Alicia Rios owns Restaurante Los Siete Jardines in Madrid, Spain, and is an acknowledged expert on garlic.

Dorothy Foster Sly holds a graduate certificate in Science Communication from the University of California, Santa Cruz, and has contributed articles to numerous professional journals, including *Professional Nutritionist*. She lives in Sonoma, California.

S. Irene Virbila is the author of *Cook's Marketplace* (101 Productions) and is a frequent contributor of food articles and restaurant reviews to major magazines and newspapers. She resides in Oakland, California.

Gratitude is expressed to those who created special garlic menus for the book: Bruce Cost, Barbara Karoff, Marti Sousanis, and Rosina Wilson. More on them with their menus.

Special thanks are owed to recipe testers and menu planners: Natasha Granoff of Aris Books did a prodigious job testing and developing these recipes, and Irene Chriss, a fine cook and teacher, did a wonderful job testing and creating recipes early on.

Heartfelt appreciation is extended to Jack Litewka, Managing Director of Aris Books. He rescued me when the heat was on, taught me the gift of word processing, and gave me the support I needed to finish. Everyone at Aris Books rooted me on, and I am grateful to them.

Thanks to Frances Bowles, Maggie Klein, and Carolyn Miller for their fine editing of this diverse project.

I would like to thank Sue Kreitzman for her book, *Garlic* (Harmony Books).

Thanks to the good folks at Simon & Schuster, who did not let the lateness of the book diminish their enthusiasm.

Much gratitude is due to The Berkeley Garlic Festival Committee for its valiant efforts.

Finally, I want to thank the membership of Lovers of the Stinking Rose. Your response to the call is what this is all about. The thrill of receiving your letters, recipes, poems, and stories has not subsided. It's all so wonderfully crazy that one must suspect, like the ancients, that garlic is divinely endowed with special powers.

L. John Harris

Introduction

≈ L. JOHN HARRIS ≈

Garlic is a fun, funny, and fundamental food. It is neither a spice, herb, nor vegetable. It is all three. It is not only culinary in its use, but also medicinal and metaphorical. Garlic inspires a festive spirit, creates a sense of groundedness, and unites people in a spirit of camaraderie. Garlic is basic to all the world's best cooking—there are very few exceptions—and is one of the most written-about foods. Garlic is musical in its ability to create a lively yet deep register on the palate. Waverly Root, the great food writer, referred to garlic as the "tuba" of the spice orchestra, and like the tuba, garlic gets ridiculed for its rotund culinary reverberations. Such is life. Such is garlic.

Garlic is also a mysterious food, separated from its original ancestor by centuries of cultivation and naturalization all over the world. Garlic is a religious symbol, and has been used for a variety of rituals and sacraments in ancient cultures. The list of its attributes is endless, and thus the literature on garlic is endless as well.

What is exciting, I think, about this book of all new material on my favorite food, is that it represents a real leap in sophistication. *The Book of Garlic* was written and assembled from the point of view of a delirious novice just discovering the pleasures and mysteries of *Allium sativum*. In the decade following publication of the book, a club was formed—Lovers of the Stinking Rose (LSR)—and a newsletter published—*Garlic Times*. With clove firmly in cheek, the American Garlic Revolution zoomed forward with each passing year. Garlic festivals began to sprout like garlic bulbs, and a literature of garlic began to take shape: articles in food and lifestyle magazines, newspaper food sections, and medical journals; films on garlic; contributions to the *Garlic Times* newsletter—15 issues worth; scholarly papers presented at an Oxford symposium on gastronomy; and books on garlic (see Garlic Bibliography, page 116).

Although the garlic clove that I carry between my teeth and cheek is permanently implanted, the fact remains that garlic is still one of the most important foods in America, and a certain cloud of purpose has settled over the key players in this culinary subculture. *The Offical Garlic Lovers Handbook* is,

then, a collection of garlic-related materials for the serious garlic lover. But lest the pendulum swing too far in the purposeful direction, this second book of garlic has its share of garlic-inspired silliness. Yet I no longer care to convince the alliophobe that garlic is really a funny, yummy food. *The Book of Garlic* plays that role and has a life of its own. With translations in about a half-dozen languages, *The Book of Garlic* is like a missionary, off to remote areas seeking converts. *The Offical Garlic Lovers Handbook* is for the lover of the stinking rose, who no longer needs to be persuaded that garlic is "as good as ten mothers."

Today's garlic eaters know that garlic is good for them. No one needs to tell them about garlic's healthful benefits. Yet the last decade has also brought more convincing research into garlic's health properties, and Part IV, Garlic: The Medicine, summarizes this research.

We no longer need to hear that garlic can be added in great quantities without overwhelming the palate, so the idea of another collection of garlic recipes with lots of hints and tips seemed unnecessary. I had collected dozens of recipes from garlic festivals, chefs, LSR club members, and friends, and those of us testing the recipes decided that it would be more interesting to create complete garlic menus. Every meal could be a little garlic festival! In addition, I asked some specialists to give us menus featuring garlic from various garlicky cultures.

The Offical Garlic Lovers Handbook makes a departure from the usual journalistic approach to garlic in one other area. Several of the contributions were first offered at the Oxford Symposium on Science, Tradition, and Superstition in the Kitchen, organized in 1985 by British food authority Alan Davidson. For the British to acknowledge the relevance of garlic in gastronomy is truly a revolution! (More on this in Part I, Garlic: Past and Present.)

I hope that *The Offical Garlic Lovers Handbook* will please in its own way as much as *The Book of Garlic* pleased. They are intended to be companion volumes. If this new collection of garlic expressions does provide pleasure, then I hope it will also inspire response. For I have little doubt that with the help of veteran as well as new Lovers of the Stinking Rose, another, even more elevated collection will find its way into print.

A Clove of Garlic Is a Metaphor

Here is the cramped boat
your ancestors came to this country in
with their spiced kielbasa and
unpronounceable hopes
And here is the small wax
lantern that burns for you
at its green center:
you who stole away when mommy wasn't looking
to a far aisle in the A&P
marked *Adult Tastes*,
never to be heard from again.

Dorothy Barresi
Amherst, MA

Having recently read *The Book of Garlic* in Japanese translation, I was pleasantly surprised to learn there are so many enthusiastic lovers of garlic in the United States.... Does this mean that the United States is advanced in everything?

Toshio Hanajima
Tokyo, Japan

GARLIC

Past and Present

THE FOLLOWING review of garlic's history by Alexandra Hicks is succinct and authoritative. Ms. Hicks presented a paper on garlic, entitled "The Mystique of Garlic," at the Oxford Symposium, held in 1985. I am delighted to be able to include excerpts of it here. I consider it quite official . . . and the perfect place to begin.

The Official Story

≈ ALEXANDRA H. HICKS ≈

WHAT IS an herb?" the eighth-century scholar Alcuin inquired of Charlemagne. "The friend of physicians and the praise of cooks," replied the great emperor.

A more appropriate and succinct description of garlic is hard to find. One of the oldest herbs used by mankind for food, for flavoring and for medicine, garlic fits the description perfectly. There is no question as to why garlic was among the 68 plants that Charlemagne listed in his *Capitulare de Villis Imperialibus* and decreed that his subjects grow in their gardens.

That garlic (*Allium sativum L.*), which is found in the genus *Allium* (along with some 500 other species), has been grown in gardens in most parts of the world since the beginning of recorded history cannot be debated. Our earliest records reveal that it was already domesticated at the time when early civilizations were developing their different forms of writing, and that it played a central role in the history of diet, folk medicine, and in the beliefs and rituals of early religions where it was simultaneously worshipped as a god and scorned as an associate of the devil.

That it has survived for some 5,000 years as a distinct species is not surprising. One of the two best-known members of the amaryllis family (the other being the onion), garlic has an underground bulb that allows it to store food. This reserve, in turn, allows garlic to survive periods of drought, etc., when many other plants would succumb. Another advantage is that it contains antifungal and antibiotic principals which could offer the garlic plant protection against bulb decay. Furthermore, the garlic bulb emits a very strong, pungent odor the moment it is eaten, which would serve as a repellent to many insects and animals who would otherwise eat and destroy it. The foliage also contains a pungent odor and taste that many predators find repulsive.

Early man, however, seemingly was attracted to this plant, rather than repelled, and realizing but not fully understanding its many virtues, used and treated it both with awe and respect.

Who first brought this plant into the garden is difficult to answer. Undoubtedly, the cultivation of garlic began in the remote past, long before the dawn of history. Although various authors write of wild garlic as being found in various parts of the world, botanists deny the fact and claim that no known wild forms of *Allium sativum* exist.* The species name *sativum* actually means "cultivated." A plant so constantly cultivated and so easily propagated may spread from gardens and persist for a considerable time without being wild by nature.

Its range of distribution is large and encompasses the Old World centers of early agricultural development and plant domestication in western Asia and China. Its exact place of origin is difficult to ascertain. DeCandolle, in his treatise *The Origin of Cultivated Plants,* considers that it was most likely indigenous to the southwest of Siberia, and most botanists agree as to its location in western Asia. It has also been considered that garlic was brought via Asia Minor to Mesopotamia and Egypt by nomadic tribes and from there back up through India via the trade routes to eastern Asia and westward to Europe. Today it is naturalized all over the world.

---

* *This is true; however, garlic-flavored bulbs do exist in the wild—the most common in North America being* Allium canadense. (*—Ed.*)

Historical Aspects

The records of the great nations of antiquity—the Sumerians, Assyrians, Egyptians, Persians, Indians, and Chinese—reveal interesting information about the important roles that garlic played in their cultures. Garlic was unquestionably highly praised and highly regarded by most people, but scorned and even condemned by others. The array of powers ascribed to garlic are very impressive. It has ranged from being worshipped as a god to being labeled an agent of the devil! However, regardless of whether they loved or hated it, ancient peoples recognized its virtues as a food and a flavoring and, above all, as a medicine.

Mesopotamia

The information that we glean from the clay tablets of Mesopotamia, "the cradle of civilization," is not only the earliest but, to the author, some of the most exciting from a culinary point of view. Decipherment of the cuneiform symbols revealed that the Mesopotamians were great users of garlic. It played an important part in their medicine and held a special place on their tables, including the tables of the kings. In the records of the royal kings we find that foodstuffs were delivered to the courts in great quantities, and garlic was no exception. Although garlic was listed as one of the plants grown in the royal gardens, it obviously was not enough to fulfill royal needs. The most interesting fact regarding the Babylonian tablets is that, unlike some other ancient records which do not contain any recipes (or dwell at any length on cuisine), the Babylonian tablets contain some culinary recipes, although admittedly most are medicinal formulas.

Recently, scholars at Yale University discovered that three Akkadian tablets, dating to approximately 1700 B.C., which originally were thought to have contained pharmaceutical formulas, were actually collections of culinary recipes. These 4,000-year-old recipes have revealed a cuisine of striking richness, sophistication, refinement, and artistry. There appears to be a strong emphasis on aromatic meat stews, and garlic, onions, and leeks are favored seasonings—although mint, juniper berries, mustard, coriander, and cumin were also used.

Egypt

Unfortunately, the Egyptians left very scanty records regarding food and food preparation and no recipes whatsoever. We can only surmise what the ancient Egyptian cuisine was like and what they ate from evidence that we have found in their tombs and pyramids and from the writings of others, such as the Greek historian, Herodotus. In the fifth century B.C., Herodotus noted that he saw an inscription in Egyptian characters on the Great Pyramid of King Cheops, which, according to his interpreter, recorded the quantity of radishes, onions, and garlic eaten by the workmen who built it and the money spent for their purchase (said to be 1,600 talents of silver). This inscription no longer exists, but Egyptian words in other inscriptions are interpreted as referring to onion, leek, and garlic.

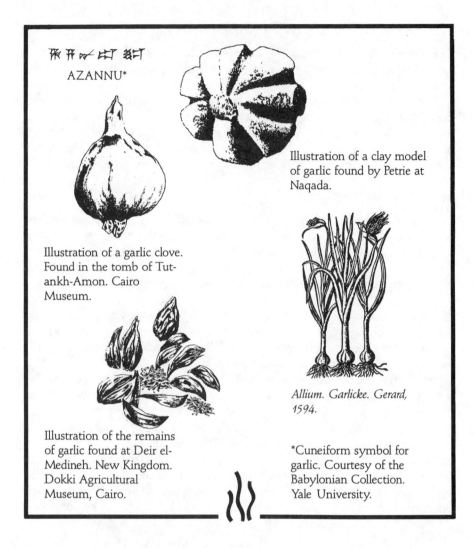

AZANNU*

Illustration of a clay model of garlic found by Petrie at Naqada.

Illustration of a garlic clove. Found in the tomb of Tut-ankh-Amon. Cairo Museum.

Allium. Garlicke. Gerard, 1594.

Illustration of the remains of garlic found at Deir el-Medineh. New Kingdom. Dokki Agricultural Museum, Cairo.

*Cuneiform symbol for garlic. Courtesy of the Babylonian Collection. Yale University.

Herodotus also noted that the Egyptians made great use of garlic. Pliny, the first-century Roman historian, wrote that in ancient Egypt garlic and onions were esteemed as gods and that the Egyptians took their oaths upon them.

Jewish tradition also testifies to the cultivation of garlic in Egypt. When the children of Israel wandered hungrily in the desert, they recalled with longing the appetizing foods of Egypt, which included garlic. "We remember the fish, which we did eat in Egypt freely; the cucumbers, and the melons, and the leeks, and the onions, and the garlick." (Numbers 11:5)

The finding of bulbs of garlic with their stems, leaves, and flowers is evidence of its cultivation in Egypt: imported bulbs would not have had leaves and flowers.

Garlic was highly esteemed, as is evidenced by the bulbs of garlic found in a New Kingdom tomb at Deir el-Medineh (see figure), in Tut-ankh-Amon's tomb, and in several others.

Besides the organic garlic that was interred with the kings, clay models dating from before 3000 B.C., have been found in the Pre-Dynastic cemeteries of Al-Mahasna and Nagada.

The various papyri also reveal much information: from the Harris papyrus we learn that Ramses III distributed garlic to the temples in great quantities, and from the *Codex Ebers*, a medical papyrus dating to about 1550 B.C., we find that 22 formulas recommend garlic for a variety of problems including heart problems, worms, throat tumors, and headaches. Many other texts recommend garlic for the same and other ailments.

Besides its use in food, medicine, and religion, garlic was an important material in the Egyptian process of mummification and helped preserve many a body for posterity. This use can now be explained because of garlic's anti-fungal property, which prevents decay.

The worship of garlic had an adverse effect on the priests, who intensely disliked the foul-smelling god of the people and refused to allow anyone who smelled of garlic into their temples.

Ancient Israel

We have already seen that the ancient Israelites were very fond of garlic, which they had eaten in great quantities while under bondage in Egypt, and it seems that this fondness has prevailed throughout their history.

In the Hebrew *Talmud* (the code of Jewish religious and civil law) we read that many foods are regularly seasoned with garlic, and it remains a favorite seasoning with Jewish people today. According to the *Talmud*, the eating of garlic served many purposes: it satiated hunger, it kept the body warm, it brightened up the face, it killed parasites in the body, and it removed jealousy and fostered love. Most interesting of all is the fact that the *Talmud* approves of garlic as an aphrodisiac, and recommends the eating of garlic on Friday—Friday being the night that was to be devoted to conjugal love, and garlic seemed like a good stimulant.

Ancient China

The *Calendar of the Hsia*, a Chinese text dating back to 2000 B.C., mentions garlic—which means that the Chinese have known and grown garlic for at least 4,000 years. According to some scholars, the Chinese characters used for writing the word *suan*, the Chinese name for *Allium sativum*, indicate that it is an herb that has been known for a long time.

Chinese traditional medicine dates back to early times; garlic, with its many medicinal virtues, was highly regarded in their pharmacopeias. Among

its many attributes, garlic was thought to purify water and to destroy the nox-
ious effect of meat and fish. The latter use is supported by a passage found in
the *Travels of Marco Polo*. When Marco Polo was passing through the Yunnan in
the thirteenth century, he observed the people eating raw meat and noted, "The
poore sort go to the Shambles and take the raw liver as soon as it is drawn from
the beasts; then they chop it up small, put it in garlic sauces, and eat it there
and then. And then they do likewise with every other kind of flesh."

The Chinese use of garlic with flesh was astute in view of the fact that
modern research has shown that the antimicrobial factor in garlic preserves
meat and keeps it fresh from two to four times longer than unpreserved meat.

Garlic has always been one of the key flavorings in Chinese cuisine and
still is so today, especially in Shantung Province.

Ancient India

In general, garlic was considered a valuable food and medicine in ancient India,
while at the same time it was believed that the odor of garlic portrayed the
presence of evil spirits. Because it was thought that the effects and taste of garlic
turned the pious away from spiritual thinking, it was shunned by the Brahman
class.

Ancient Greece

It is from the classical texts of the ancient Greeks and Romans that we derive
our greatest amount of *materia medica* and botanical information. Most of our
English herbals are based on the writings of Greek physicians (such as Hippocrates and Dioscorides) and philosophers (such as Aristotle and Theophrastus). Theophrastus (372–280 B.C.), a pupil of Aristotle, was one of the first to
try to establish a scientific system of plants. His books, based on Aristotle's
botanical writings and his own observations, contain some rather interesting
information on garlic. Among many other observations he notes "that the
sweetness of taste, smell, and vigor [of garlica bulbs] depend on their cultivation
and position in the garden" and "that stored garlic appears to have the most
pungent smell at the season when those in the ground are sprouting," adding
that sprouting, which takes place in both, is the result of a latent force stirring
garlic into action. He also mentions a type of garlic called Cyprian, which was
not cooked but used in salads.

Hippocrates (460–337 B.C.), known as "the father of medicine" and the
author of the Hippocratic Oath, left extensive records of botanicals; his advice,
"Let food be your medicine," is often quoted today. He used garlic for many
things, including the treatment of infections, wounds, and intestinal disorders.

Dioscorides, a Greek physician of the first century A.D. who travelled with
the Roman army and whose *Materia Medica* was the authoritative source for
physicians for the next 1,500 years, highly recommended garlic for many
things—e.g., clearing the arteries and getting rid of intestinal worms. He also
wrote that it dulled the eyesight.

Garlic was also an element in the practice of Greek magic. Theophrastus wrote that garlic was placed on stones at crossroads as an offering to Hecate, the goddess of magic, witchcraft, sorcery, and enchantment; and Homer states that Ulysses owed his narrow escape from being changed into an animal (by the enchantress Circe) to the virtues of garlic. Greek root gatherers, know as *rhizotomi*, smeared themselves with garlic oil or ate a lot of garlic before gathering hellebore, a poisonous plant, possibly as a protection against its poisonous juices.

Even though some Greeks were known to have collected recipes, very few have survived. Brief references to food are found in "Deipnosophists" ("The Learned Banquet") by Athenaeus of Naucratis, who wrote in the second century. Garlic was served as a food at banquets, as is shown by his description of an Attic banquet: "They place upon the table a large platter holding five smaller plates within its space, one full of garlic, while another holds two boil'd sea urchins . . . ."

We also learn about food from Aristophanes (448–380 B.C.), the greatest of the Greek comic dramatists, who mentions garlic in his plays many times. In *Lysistrata*, in which the women rebel against their warrior husbands, Cynnali says to Acestor, "If you come near me I swear you will never eat either garlic or black beans again."

However, we know that garlic was not a favorite food with everyone. Although the common and rural people consumed much garlic, the aristocratic element frowned upon its odor and refrained from eating it, lest they be thought to be common. Cybele, mother of the gods of Olympus, disliked the smell so much that she refused entrance to her temple to all those who smelled of garlic.

Ancient Rome

In ancient Rome, as in Greece, garlic was frowned upon by the aristocracy, who rejected it because of its foul odor. However, they fully realized its many virtues and much approved it as a food for their soldiers, sailors, and athletes— all of whom were fed quantities of garlic daily to increase their strength, energy, stamina, vitality, and endurance. It was also believed that garlic excited the courage of warriors: to ensure excellence of performance, ample provision of garlic was always made for all military expeditions, both on land and at sea. The military Romans became such believers in the benefits of garlic that they took it with them everywhere they went, and it was the Roman legions that introduced garlic to many of the peoples they conquered, especially those of northern Europe.

Olympic athletes partook freely of garlic, particularly during their arduous training. For the same reasons, garlic was fed to game cocks before fights.

Garlic was also fed by the nobles to their laborers, especially to those who labored in the fields under the hot sun. According to Virgil, it was believed that garlic gave strength during periods of great heat.

Like the Greeks before them, the ancient Romans believed that the effects of foul air were neutralized by garlic—and this is possibly another reason why the workers, peasants, and rural population used garlic so lavishly that it became known as the "physic of the peasantry."

Galen (131–200 A.D.), a Roman physician who was Greek by birth, had so many uses for garlic that he called it *Theriaca Rusticoriam*, meaning the "common person's *theriake"—theriake* being a honey-based, paste-like medicinal preparation effective against poisons. In English, *Theriaca Rusticoriam* became "poor man's treacle" and in French it became "theriaque de pauvres."

Pliny was also a great believer in garlic as a medicine, and he listed 61 garlic remedies in his *Natural History*. His remedies include the use of garlic for hemorrhoids, bruises, skin ulcers, blisters, asthma, dropsy, jaundice, toothache, earache, catarrh, hoarseness, coughs, and intestinal parasites. In cases of leprosy and eruptions of the skin, he believed that it could act as a deterrent and effect a cure and that garlic beaten with fresh coriander and taken in pure wine acted as an aphrodisiac. Adverse effects of garlic mentioned included dimness of the sight.

De Re Coquinara (*Of Things Culinary*), a cookbook compiled by Apicius, reputedly a Roman gourmet in the fourth century A.D., is the only extant cookbook containing recipes of this period. Because it was compiled by a gourmet obviously for use in the kitchens of the nobles, garlic is not used in any of the recipes. This verifies the Roman aristocrat's disdain for garlic as opposed to the Roman commoner's appreciation of it. Roman recipes containing garlic would thus indicate a rural origin. Carbonized remains of garlic have been found at Herculaneum.

Historical Aspects—Medieval to Modern Times

The Dark and Middle Ages that followed the collapse of the Roman Empire produced very little literature from which we can extract with any exactness the use of garlic during that period. We know that it continued to be important for both food and medicine from sources such as the Plan of St. Gall, intended as the ideal plan for the structure and operation of the Benedictine Monasteries. The list of recommended garden plants included garlic, which was to be grown by itself in a rectangular plot within a larger garden.

In Europe, only the monasteries kept alive the literature of medical and herbal practices. The monks became the physicians and healers, and the sick sought and got aid from them. Garlic was, for instance, the specific agent against leprosy, and lepers became known as "pilgarlics"—because they were given whole garlic, which they had to peel (*pil*) themselves. They used garlic as a medication, relying on herbals such as Dioscorides' *Materia Medica* for guidance.

Introduced earlier by the conquering Romans, garlic was grown in most medieval gardens throughout northern Europe, and it, along with onions, leeks, and chives, was plentiful and cheap. All of these foods were much used in medieval kitchens, where they satisfied cravings for robust flavors and bewitching smells. Everyone could afford them and everyone used them, especially people who could not afford the more expensive spices. These foods were stewed, fried, eaten raw (with bread and cheese), or pounded into sauces. The large quantity of garlic, pounded and put into sauces, inspired the motto, "The mortar always smells of garlic."

In England, the use of garlic in cookery prevailed even after the Romans departed. The Anglo-Saxons grew and used the form of garlic (*Allium sativum*) that the Romans had brought to England, as if they had had it all along. Although the Anglo-Saxons cannot be given the credit for its introduction, they must be given credit for its name. Garlic, the prevailing common name for *Allium sativum*, is derived directly from the Anglo-Saxon *gar* (meaning "spear") and *leac* (meaning "leek"). Leeks, members of the same family as garlic, grew wild in Britain. The name *garlic* thus means a plant with spearlike leaves that resembles a leek. The genus name, *Allium*, prevails from the Romans and is the old Latin name for garlic.

Food and feasting were among the main diversions of medieval society. Copious quantities of ingeniously prepared food (like their Roman predecessors, medieval chefs liked to display their ingenuity) were heavily spiced and strongly flavored. One wonders if spices, including garlic, weren't used in medieval times as much for their stimulating effects as for their flavoring and preservative effects. There is no question that after one eats garlic, a warm, invigorating feeling prevails throughout the whole system. Once coffee, tea, and other stimulants arrived on the scene, the heavy spicing of food declined.

Perusing the old cookery books of the period is enlightening. A good example is *The Forme of Cury*, a cookbook compiled by the chief master cooks of Richard II in 1390. The foreword states that it was written with "the assent and advisement of the masters of physic and philosophy that dwell in the King's Court." The colophon asserts, "*Explicit coquina que est optima medicina.*" ("Here concludes the art of cookery, which is the best medicine.")

It appears that cookery manuscripts such as this one and others were written from a point of view that a good cuisine is the best insurance for health; therefore, it stands to reason that ingredients were chosen as much for their health-giving properties as for their flavor. Garlic, being both health-giving and flavor-imparting, would have been popular.

Recipes in *The Forme of Cury* show that garlic was used in a variety of ways:

> Aquapatys: Pill [peel] garlic, and cast it in a pot with water and oile, and seethe it. Do there to safron, salt, and powder-fort, and dresse it forth hool.

> Salat: Take parsel, sauge, garlic, chibollas, onyons . . . and serve it forth.

> Sauce Madame: Take sauge, parsel, ysope . . . garlek and grapes,
> and fylle the gees there with . . .

In the first recipe, garlic is served as a boiled vegetable; in the second it is served in a raw salad; and in the third it becomes a part of the dressing for a stuffed goose.

In another manuscript of the time, *Ashmole MS 2145*, we find the following recipe for garlic sauce:

> Sauce Gauncile: Take floure and cowe mylke, safroune wil y-
> ground, garleke, and put in-to a faire litel pot; and sethe it over
> the fire, and serve it forthe.

That garlic was much used and enjoyed during this period is perhaps best summed up by Chaucer, the great English poet, who in the Prologue to the *Canterbury Tales* (c. 1386) wrote, "Wel loved be garleek, onyons and lekes."

While the old classical Greek, Roman, and Arabic herbals and treatises were being copied and recopied within monastery walls, as the Middle Ages progressed, interest increased in herbal remedies. New herbals were written as a result of the intellectual revolution of the Renaissance. As observations and experiments flourished, old preconceptions slowly fell away. Uses of herbs and plants became more realistic and plant material was better illustrated. One of the first men to study plants scientifically in England was John Turner. His *New Herbal* appeared in 1551 and was well received. His work was followed by others, such as Dodens in Europe and John Gerard in England. Gerard's herbal, first printed in 1594 but revised by Johnson in 1633, proved to be extremely popular. Another extremely popular herbal in England was that of John Parkinson, whose *Paradisi in Sole, Paradise Terrestris* appeared in 1629. These herbals, which were much more comprehensive and authoritative than earlier ones, became the medical, botanical, and culinary references of the time. They not only gave plant descriptions, growing advice, and uses, but sometimes offered cookery advice as well.

Regarding garlic, Gerard writes: "Being eaten, it heateth the body extremely . . . openeth obstructions, is an enemie to all cold poysons, and to the bitings of venomous beasts; and therefore Galen nameth it *Theriaca Rusticoriam*, or the husband man's Treacle." The uses go on and on and include many which have been validated today such as: "It taketh away the roughness of the throat; it helpeth an old cold; it killeth worms in the belly." Others, such as "With fig leaves and cumin it is laid on against the bitings of the mouse called in Greeke, in English, a shrew," have, as far as I know, not been validated!

On "The Use of Garlicke" Parkinson writes, "It is accounted, and so called in diverse countries, the poure man's Treacle, that is, a remedy for all diseases. . . ."

Turner wrote that garlic "is good against all venome and poyson, taken in meats or boiled in wine and drunken, for of this own nature it with standeth all poyson. . . ." And Dodens confirms that "it can be used against all poisons. Will cure coughs and toothache. . . ."

Cole, in his *Art of Simpling*, echos some of the old Greek and Roman claims, such as "Cocks are most stout of fight, and so are horses," and another interesting use which is presently being validated in Michigan: " . . . and if the garden is infected with moles, garlic will convince them to leap out of the ground presently."

Along with the new herbals, the invention of the printing press led to an increasing number of new household-management and cookery books. Today these are interesting from several aspects, not the least of which is that they give us a good idea of the thinking about foodstuffs at the time. Although the new herbals contained as many (if not more) uses for garlic as the old herbals, the use of garlic in the recipes of the new cookery books declined. This is not to say that it fell into disfavor by everyone. A glance through the garden inventory of Hardwicke Hall shows that Bess of Hardwicke was growing it in her garden in 1601, and although in Shakespeare's *A Midsummer-Night's Dream*, we find Bottom saying, " . . . eat no onions, nor garlic, for we are to utter sweet breath"), we can be quite certain that the Shakesperean commoner was not too different from the Chaucerian commoner, who certainly enjoyed his garlic. However, Sir Hugh Platt, Robert May, Charles Carter, Richard Bradley, Joseph Cooper, and other authors of the seventeenth and eighteenth centuries find no place in their recipes for garlic, scarcely mentioning it or not mentioning it at all.

Evelyn is an exception: in his *Acetaria* he devotes more than one page to the subject of garlic, but it is clear that he thinks it fit only for the "Rustic northerns . . . or such as use the sea." He goes on to say, "Whilst we absolutely forbid it entrance into our salleting, by reason of its intolerable rankness, and which made it so detested of old; that 'tis not for ladies palates, nor those who court them, further than to permit a light touch on the dish, with a clove thereof, much better supply'd by the gentler rocambo."

It is not surprising that the upper-middle classes in Victorian England also found the rankness of garlic intolerable. Mrs. Beeton, in her *Household Management* (1861), wrote that "the smell of this plant is generally considered offensive and it is the most acrimonious in its taste of the whole alliaceous tribe." Only one recipe in her entire book—for an Indian chutney—uses garlic as an ingredient.

Interestingly, garlic became very popular in England during the First World War, when it was widely used in front-line casualty stations as an antiseptic dressing for suppurating wounds. Military doctors thought very highly of it, and in 1916, the government begged for as much garlic as could be produced and paid handsome prices for it.

In the English kitchen, however, garlic did not regain popularity until British tourists became exposed to Mediterranean cuisine. As British cuisine becomes more international, garlic is used more frequently, although not as often as in other countries, especially the Mediterranean ones, Russia, and the United States.

The Garlic Revolution Today

≈ L. JOHN HARRIS ≈

T HAT IT has taken America hundreds of years to become one of the world's garlicky cultures is curious. What forces have held down our obvious contemporary garlic lust? Anglo-Saxons are usually blamed for bringing with them to America an abhorrence of foul-smelling, peasanty garlic. But America has also absorbed French, Italian, Spanish, and numerous Asian groups who use garlic. We are a melting-pot, and the pot has lots of garlic in it.

The Mouthwash Theory

So, what powers have until now prevented garlic from taking over? I have always pointed to a kind of Anglo-Saxon conspiracy, symbolized in the 1970s by a growing mouthwash industry. In a publicity stunt planned by Lever Brothers, the large pharmaceutical company heavily invested in mouthwash products, I was flown to New York in 1977 to debate a Lever Brothers chemist on local TV on the usefulness of their mouthwash in ridding the breath of garlic odor. I tried to make the point that this temporary masking of garlic's odor was to no avail, since on the one hand the masking effect was only temporary, and on the other, the body would still emit odor from the pores, thus making a mouthwash *bath* the only effective antidote. (Reporting on this stunt in the *Washington Post*, a cartoonist drew a picture of a young man in a bathtub filled with mouthwash. I have it framed and hanging in my office. I am very proud of the cartoon, because it was this debating point that seemed to give me victory.)

While I still stand by this Anglo-Saxon theory, let's call it the mouthwash theory, another element has entered the picture which I am just now starting to see. It involves Native Americans (once commonly referred to as American Indians). Now, I know almost nothing about the evolution of our continent or the native cultures found by its colonizers. This gives me, therefore, appropriate license to speculate.

The Indian Suppression Theory

The introduction of garlic into the Americas is not nearly as well documented as are its travels along the trade routes from its home in southwestern Asia to Europe. We know that the Spanish explorers brought garlic to the Americas, but there is also a Native American tradition of garlic consumption, especially for medicinal purposes. There are many stories about wild garlic being used

This photo, from a 1956 issue of *Colliers* magazine, perfectly portrays the pre-Garlic Revolution attitude in America toward garlic: don't get too close, don't touch, and enjoy from afar. Actually, you can tell from the picture that, as a culture, we are at least beginning to acknowledge garlic's culinary perfume.

by the Native Americans to cure sick Europeans. It is also fairly clear that progressive waves of European and Asian immigrants brought a taste for garlic to Anglo-Saxon America. Many immigrants realized, however, that to assimilate and compete in the American melting pot, they would have to tone down their garlic consumption. And thus, the American mouthwash and breath-mint industry was born. But Native Americans were not allowed to assimilate. Why? I shall hazard a guess that may seem more absurd than it actually is.

Native Americans knew where the wild garlic was. The Anglo-Saxons wanted to control garlic awareness in America, knowing that garlic-loving Europeans and Asians would eventually flock to America. Perhaps the new Americans feared that the native Americans, with access to wild garlic (*Allium canadense*), would later pose a threat to their plans to cultivate *Allium sativum*. So they got nasty with the natives. For hundreds of years, therefore, the Anglo-Saxons, and their assimilated European brothers, have built the garlic industry in America to serve their own needs and those of the Asians, who love garlic too much to assimilate. Now, with two world wars under our belts, the United States has emerged as a garlic-loving country, but control of garlic is now held by an increasingly diverse lot. As the poet, William Stafford, writes in his *Ode to Garlic,* "It makes us all alike, all offspring of powerful forces, part of one great embrace of democracy . . ."

≈   ≈   ≈

One of the greatest expressions of garlic awareness is the phenomenon of the garlic festival. What is a garlic festival? Its real, symbolic meaning is as a deep, human recognition of the earth's fecundity (see Alicia Rios' essay in Part V), a ritual that reinforces our connection to earth's basic elements. With the near-elimination of the indigenous population, we not only erased North American awareness of garlic's presence, but we also lost our ritualized relationship with the earth. This is changing now, for the forces that sought to control garlic for their own purposes have, in fact, unleashed garlic awareness in North America. (I don't want to overstate garlic's role in America's culinary revolution; however, our new love of "fresh" foods, regional foods, etc., has to be seen in the same light as the Garlic Revolution—a rekindled awareness of the relationship between humans and the earth. Americans are at last starting to bond to the continent to which we are, in reality, very new. It is in this bonding that we can better understand the role garlic has to play.)

For thousands of years, garlic harvesting and eating have been celebrated at festivals all over the world. In India, Egypt, France, and Italy, garlic festivals have been recorded from ancient times to the modern era.

As early as 1938, in a cookbook called *Salads and Herbs* (J. B. Lippincott), Cora, Rose, and Bob Brown called for a Garlic Day in America:

> Garlic was so prized by the ancients that they staged a regular
> pagan festival in its honor when the new crop came in, and in
> France the custom flourishes today, with dancing in the streets,

and the hearty nibbling of whole heads of garlic as though they were apples—everything as gay as at the new wine festival in Merano. We Browns have assisted at new garlic festivals and have gone on record as favoring a Garlic Day for America—one day set aside so that everybody can enjoy this wholesome vegetable without complaining about it on the breath of anybody else.

But lovers of the stinking rose would have to wait until July 14, 1976, Bastille Day, for the first recorded garlic festival in America. At Chez Panisse Restaurant in Berkeley, California, at the urging of Lovers of the Stinking Rose, America's garlic festival tradition was born. At that first garlic festival feast (see page 50 for the recipes), garlic was served—and lots of it—in every course, including dessert.

Chez Panisse has celebrated garlic every year since then, beginning always on July 14. But in 1982, realizing that Chez Panisse could no longer satisfy the growing demand for garlic, LSR announced a city-wide festival in Berkeley, with over 25 restaurants participating. Now, The Berkeley Garlic Festival features two weeks of garlic at over 50 restaurants, as well as garlic films, dances, and other events.

Meanwhile, in 1978, garlic took another major step towards national prominence. Concluding that there was gold in them thar garlic fields, the town fathers of Gilroy, California, the self-proclaimed garlic capital of the world, launched their own garlic festival, modeled after a festival in Arleux, France. With the help of the Fresh Garlic Association, and acknowledging the trailblazing role of LSR, Gilroy invited the media to witness what would become a major new food festival in America. The rest is history: 100,000 people flock to Gilroy every year around August 1 to bask in the aroma of garlic in a countyfair atmosphere complete with music, exhibitions, cook-offs, etc.

Outside of California, festivals were cropping up like spring onions: in Washington State, a restaurant was achieving recognition as one of James Beard's favorites: The Ark. Its garlic festival began to gain momentum in the early 1980s. James Beard is often credited with the initial thrust of modern American garlic-awareness when he introduced Provençal 40-clove garlic chicken to his cookbook readers. (Julia Child shares this credit with her down-to-earth French cooking.)

Elsewhere, LSR began to note garlic-festival eruptions in Portland, Oregon; Boca Raton, Florida; Toronto, Canada; Covington, Kentucky; and Fitchburg, Massachusetts.

But the most significant garlic festival to appear in recent years is in Los Angeles. As if not to be outdone by Northern California, Los Angeles Garlic Week is a major event now, co-sponsored by a popular restaurant in L.A., Nucleus Nuance, and LSR's Southern California chapter, headed by Charles Perry. The American Red Cross is a key player in Los Angeles Garlic Week: it receives a percentage of the proceeds from the ticket sales. Combining the restaurant

In Arleux, France, the garlic-festival tradition goes back decades. The community celebrates the new garlic harvest, a queen is selected, and the entire population puts on the collective garlic feed bag. The Arleux festival is the model for the Gilroy Garlic Festival.

JOSIAH BACON

Serious garlic lovers often make spectacles of themselves, especially during garlic festivals. Like Mardis Gras in New Orleans, a garlic festival is an opportunity to express oneself. Pictured from left to right and from top to bottom: Mayor Gus Newport of Berkeley, California, officially recognizing the Berkeley Garlic Festival, L. John Harris in 1978 with his garlic memorabilia and official LSR turban, Bruce Aidells, sausage maker, Les Blank, filmmaker, Charles Perry, LSR's fearless Southern California leader.

These buttons are on display in our Garlic Museum. Some of them are available by "mail odor" from Lovers of the Stinking Rose.

orientation of The Berkeley Garlic Festival and the outdoor fair feature of the Gilroy Festival, the L.A. festival has it all: booths selling foods prepared by many of L.A.'s top restaurants in an outdoor setting complete with continuous live jazz, ceremonial presentations, contest drawings, etc. This one-night event is followed by a week of garlic menus at participating restaurants. Mayor Tom Bradley has officially recognized L.A. Garlic Week, as has California's Secretary of State, March Fong Eu.

All this accelerated garlic activity can only mean that America has rediscovered its indigenous bond with garlic and the earthly forces symbolized by garlic. And just as garlic is healthy for individuals, it is healthy for cultures as well.

Here is a listing of garlic festivals open to the public, with details of how to contact the festival for more information. Of course, LSR can always be contacted for information. We are always trying to update our festival guide—so please let us know of any festivals we have missed.

Garlic Festivals in America

Chez Panisse Garlic Festival
Berkeley, California (est. 1976)

Date: July 14-(varies). Reservations needed (often sold out far in advance).

Special Events: All-garlic menus, live music, and dancing.

For more information: Call Chez Panisse at (415) 548-5525, or call LSR at (415) 527-5171.

Gilroy Garlic Festival
Gilroy, California (est. 1978)

A county-fair atmosphere with all the trimmings: contests, exhibitions, dances, a garlic golf tournament, and dozens of food booths.

Date: Last weekend in July.

For more information: Call the Gilroy Garlic Festival at (408) 842-1625, or write Gilroy Garlic Festival, P.O. Box 2311, Gilroy, CA 95020. (NOTE: Do *not* call LSR for information on the Gilroy Festival—we'd be swamped! But we do announce the dates of the festival in our newsletter.)

The Berkeley Garlic Festival
Berkeley, California (est. 1982)

Over 50 East Bay restaurants feature garlic on their menus for up to two weeks, beginning on Bastille Day.

Date: July 14-(varies).

Special Events: Film festival, garlic dance, mini-festivals at various restaurants, including Chez Panisse (see Chez Panisse above).

Sponsors: LSR, The Berkeley Garlic Festival Committee, participating restaurants in the East Bay.

For more information: Call LSR at (415) 527 5171, or write LSR, 1621 Fifth Street, Berkeley, CA 94710.

The Ark Restaurant Garlic Festival
Nahcotta, Washington (est. 1982)

This annual event has spread beyond the restaurant, and the community of Nahcotta has rallied to the call. The festival draws on visitors from the Seattle area. There are full-course garlic dinners, over 50 vendors, and a band.

Date: Late June or early July.

For more information: Call The Ark Restaurant at (206) 665-4133, or write The Ark Restaurant, P.O. Box 95, Nahcotta, WA 98637.

Fitchburg Garlic Festival
Fitchburg, Massachusetts (est. 1982)

Another community event, held at an Italian church just 50 miles from Boston. The booths serve great food.

Date: Early in June.

For more information: Call Rev. Pat Biscardi at (617) 342-1290.

Los Angeles Garlic Week
Los Angeles, California (est. 1983)

An outdoor, one-night festival with food booths by L.A.'s best restaurants, live jazz, contests, presentations, and more. LSR's information booth is manned by Charles Perry, LSR's Southern California chapter leader. Participating restaurants continue the week with garlic specials.

Date: Varies. Mid to late July.

Sponsors: Nucleus Nuance restaurant and Lovers of the Stinking Rose, in conjunction with The American Red Cross.

For more information: Call Al Cranis of the Olive Company at (213) 931-1812, or write Los Angeles Garlic Week, 6472 Colgate Avenue, Los Angeles, CA 90048. Also, contact LSR.

Guilford Garlic Jamboree
Guilford, Vermont (est. 1983)

This community garlic celebration features a Garlic Potluck.

Date: Summer solstice weekend in June.

For more information: Call Honey Loring at (802) 254-2253.

Garlic Fest
Covington, Kentucky (est. 1985)

This festival near Cincinnati, Ohio, is modeled after Gilroy's, complete with a recipe cook-off, bulb-peeling contest, Miss Garlic contest, and a showing of Les Blank's *Garlic Is As Good As Ten Mothers.*

Date: Early in February.

Sponsor: Mick Noll's Covington Haus.

For more information: Write Covington Haus, 100 West Sixth Street, Covington, KY 41011, or call (606) 261-6655.

Although the garlic-festival phenomenon is now national, California is still the garlic-festival capital of America. It is possible to "festival hop" between Berkeley, Los Angeles, and Gilroy, and by including The Ark Restaurant Garlic Festival in Washington, you have a West Coast garlic-festival tour. LSR is working to coordinate dates to facilitate the tour.

FLOWER FILMS PRESENTS

GARLIC IS GOOD AS

and OTHER FILMS by LES BLANK

Les Blank's delightful film has been shown all over the world to enthusiastic audiences. Made between 1976 and 1980, the film is a virtual documentary of the Garlic Revolution at its birth, featuring scenes in Chez Panisse restaurant, Gilroy, private homes of garlic lovers, and much more.

Garlic is a peculiar plant

It wears neither skirt nor pant
It lives without sex
which is quite a hex
on an herb that would like to
—but can't.

Dr. O. Silberstein
Gilroy Foods, California

It occurred to me while reading your book that one of the likely associations of garlic is the superficial resemblance of the garlic bulb and its contents to the scrotum. This might be particularly true of some varieties which you describe as having a few large cloves....

Tom Hursh
Berkeley, CA

GARLIC

The Plant

AMERICAN cooks increasingly use fresh garlic in place of various convenience products such as dehydrated powder, commercial purées, and pre-minced or pre-slivered garlic. The flavor of fresh garlic has not, as yet, been duplicated by any processing techniques I know of. Because garlic oxidizes so readily when it is cut, commercial products must add other substances such as citric acid and/or oil to preserve them. This alters the wonderfully distinct flavor of garlic. It is no wonder then that most good cooks have moved away from processed garlic products.

Now that lovers of the stinking rose have turned almost exclusively to fresh garlic, the question becomes how to identify the many varieties of garlic in the market, and how to grow these in home gardens. Like the other culinary herbs, garlic is easy to grow. It can be harvested for either the bulb or the green shoots, and it can be picked young or fully mature.

What follows is the best overview of garlic varieties and growing instructions I have yet seen. Susan Chamberlin has interviewed many of the most knowledgeable authorities in the field, and she has resolved a lot of horticultural and botanical riddles regarding garlic and its relatives.

The Garlic Source Calendar will let you know what's up and coming throughout the year.

A Gardener's Companion: Identifying and Growing Garlic
≈ SUSAN CHAMBERLIN ≈

G ARLIC IS one of the 97 kitchen plants mentioned in a poem that is the earliest original English treatise on gardening. Written in 1440, Jon Gardener's "The Feate of Gardening" gives practical advice, and that is what this chapter is for: to provide you with practical advice for identifying and growing garlic, and with enough botanical and horticultural information so you will succeed.

Why grow garlic? To supply your kitchen with wonderful and rare varieties at their peak of freshness, to be able to make your own garlic braids, for the satisfaction of producing something useful and edible from the soil, and to protect your garden—garlic is a natural bug repellent.

Botany (the study of plant life) and horticulture (the art of growing plants) are allied. To know a plant intimately makes it easier to grow, but it is not essential to study botany. Trial and error in growing plants is all it takes. Gardening is an art that embraces both science and intuition.

Allium sativum

Many consider garlic the most important flavoring discovery that humans have ever made. It is a hardy perennial bulb that is grown as an annual, harvested, dried, and cured. The bulbs form cloves, but sometimes a "round" (or large single clove) is all that develops. White flowers appear atop naked stalks, if they appear at all, and the leaves are long and narrow and smell like garlic/onions. Seed is rarely produced, and it is sterile.

Variations on a theme. People have been growing garlic all over the world for thousands of years, so it is not surprising that there are many varieties of *Allium sativum*. It is an extremely "variable" species: distinctly different strains, called clones, commonly turn up. These could be called "variations on a theme." Each has its own virtues.

Estimates of the number of true horticultural varieties range from 30 to over 300, but some authorities insist there is no acceptable way to recognize and distinguish individual varieties with certainty. One of the few exceptions is the botanical variety *Ophioscorodon*, which is commonly known as rocambole or serpent garlic. It is described in the cultivars section that follows. Most strains are technically just selections of a few recognized basic types. In France, for example, 'Perle d'Auvergne' was selected from 'Rose d'Auvergne' and given a new name because it could be certified as disease-free.

Exactly the same variety may be grown and known by several common names in different countries or even in neighboring gardens. Nurseries often re-name varieties obtained from other sources. Some of these new names are legitimate because selections of the best of the strain have been made based on subtle or obvious differences. Nurseries also simplify to the other extreme, calling all garlics they grow *Allium sativum*, or all their white garlics "silverskin." Each may have its own character, and that is part of the fun of growing it yourself. Some poor keepers (those that do not last long in storage) with great flavor are only available from nurseries or specialty growers because supermarkets refuse to stock them. It can be very difficult to locate true, recognized cultivars.

A "cultivar" is a named cultivated variety, or *culti-var*. These names are traditionally capitalized and enclosed within single quotes, although this notation is not carefully followed outside of plant-enthusiast circles. Cultivar names remain the same; common names are not standardized and are not capitalized (unless they are proper nouns). Some cultivar names are so common they are no longer capitalized.

Three cultivars of garlic are grown on virtually all of the thousands of acres planted to garlic in California. These three varieties are: late (or 'California Late'), early (or 'California Early'), and Creole (or 'Creole'). Four other primary types are also grown in California. Most other commercial varieties available in this country are in some way related to this basic seven. Their origins span the globe. 'Chileno' (or 'Chilleno') and 'Formosan' are grown in desert and southern regions. Both are very similar to Creole. 'Egyptian' is also grown in these areas. Chilean is not widely distributed here. These four and Creole are important because they can be grown in warm southern climates.

Perhaps more important for flavor than growing an exotic variety is choosing a variety that is suited to your climate and practicing good growing and harvesting techniques. (Proper storage in a cool, dry place is also essential.) It is difficult to obtain named cultivars. Most garlic suppliers sell the 'Early' cultivar simply as "garlic" because it will succeed in many climates and latitudes. If your latitude is extremely northern or if you live in a subtropical area, try to patronize a local nursery that is raising its own locally adapted strain.

Garlic Cultivars

'California Late': Commonly called late garlic or California white garlic, this is the classic white garlic head. It is California's most valuable commercial variety, the one that dominates plantings around Gilroy in the Salinas Valley. Valued both for its color and for its long-keeping quality, it is probably the best keeper available—strong flavor, high solid content, and firm smooth bulbs. Cloves vary in color from light pink to deep red and are sheathed in white. Distinguished from all other varieties by this white clove sheathing and by its dark green, narrow, upright leaves, it is one of the garlics that is most sensitive to day length. Because bulbs will not form unless the plant is grown where its requirements for daylight are satisfied, its use as a crop is confined to a small latitude and climatic range. Late garlic is not well adapted to southern or desert areas.

'California Early': Its common name, early garlic, derives from the fact that this variety matures approximately one month before late garlic. Of all major commercial varieties, this one produces the highest average yield and the largest plants, but the bulbs do not store quite as well as late garlic and have a lower content of solids. Also, in comparison to the late, early garlic leaves are lighter or paler green, broader, and more spreading. The plants are vigorous, and the bulbs are very large, somewhat flat, and slightly rougher than late bulbs. They are composed of large, asymmetrically arranged cloves, each covered with a yellowish or pinkish-yellow protective skin. The entire bulb is covered by a sheathing that is off-white and occasionally veined with purple. Easy to grow and much less fussy about day length, this variety is grown more widely than late garlic. It is grown in California's desert valleys and wherever weather conditions are marginal for garlic production. This is the variety most often available from seed companies.

'Creole': This important cultivar, commonly called Creole, is classified as an early type and is grown primarily in hot climates. Creole is a major crop in Louisiana (where it probably originated from 'Spanish Rojo'), in Mexico, and in South America. Its value lies in the fact that it is not day-length sensitive, and as a result, it can be grown in any climate or latitude. In California, it is grown primarily in the Imperial or Palo Verde valleys. It matures about one month before 'California Early.' These seasonal advantages are more important than the bulbs it produces. They are full of various sizes of cloves randomly arranged. Some are large, but most are rather small, and many doubles (two cloves in one sheathing) occur. They are delicious, nevertheless. Each clove is covered with a dark pink or purple skin. Slightly taller and a lighter green in color, the plants are otherwise very similar to late garlic in appearance. One interesting characteristic of this variety is the seed stem it often produces. Sometimes it sends up a flower that may grow as high as 3 feet. Or, the stem may never emerge from the bulb and can often be found as part of the bulb after harvest. Its keeping quality is not quite as good as late garlic, but it is better than early garlic.

'Chileno' (or 'Chilleno'): This is an improved strain of Creole that resembles it but has better-shaped bulbs of larger cloves. It is grown in the southern interior valleys of California and adapted wherever Creole can be found.

'Chilean': Probably a descendant of 'Spanish Rojo,' this variety originated in South America, possibly in Chile. Strains of the Chilean type are also grown in Spain, India, Japan, and Formosa. It matures quickly (one or two weeks later than Creole), so it is classified as an early type, but it is very day-length sensitive and environmental requirements are quite specific as a result. The plants are larger than Creole and have flattened white bulbs with dark pink to wine-colored cloves. The cloves are even in size and arranged symmetrically around a thick central seed stem. This arrangement is like the segments of a tangerine. Each clove is about the same size and has a sharp inner edge.

'Egyptian': Averaging about 2 feet tall, this very large and fast-maturing plant is commonly called Egyptian garlic. Its large white bulbs contain many small elongated cloves covered with white skin. It is grown in California's southern interior valleys and desert regions, and is adapted wherever Creole is found.

'Italian': Italian is both a cultivar name and a common name. The named cultivar is grown in Louisiana and in other subtropical areas. Its pink or purplish cloves are stronger in flavor and smaller than Creole, the other major Louisiana type. The bulbs bear a resemblance to an artichoke. Their cloves, which are arranged like artichoke leaves, have thin outer wrappers that come off easily. Compared to Creole, the plants have narrower, lighter green leaves.

Italian is also a common name given to garlic strains that are very pungent in flavor. Not all garlics called Italian will necessarily be adapted to subtropical areas, nor are all like the named cultivar in appearance.

Allium sativum var. Ophioscorodon: Commonly called rocambole, serpent garlic, and top-setting garlic, this is a true botanical variety of *Allium sativum*. It is frequently confused with *Allium scorodoprasum*, commonly known as sand leek. In this book *rocambole* is the name for a garlic with light purple (not white) flower buds enclosed in sharply pointed green or white membranes that top tall, looping green stems called "scapes." The coiled appearance of the scapes gives this plant its more descriptive common name, serpent garlic—the literal translation of *Ophioscorodon* from the Greek.

Bulbs form underground with about six to eight cloves arranged around the flower stalk like segments of a tangerine. The bulbs are smaller than plain garlic, but they are just as pungent, and the cloves can be used in exactly the same way. They are particularly popular in French Canadian dishes.

An added bonus is the cluster of bulbils, or baby bulbs, that develop on the scapes after the pretty flowers fade. They can be eaten fresh or pickled. Great in salads, it is not necessary to peel them. These tiny round purplish bulbils can be used to propagate the plant, and like the bulbs need to be stored in a cool, dry place.

The serpent-garlic plants are smaller than garlic plants, with dark green leaves about ⅓ inch wide. Believed to have originated in Asia Minor and southeastern Europe, the scientific name for this plant includes Dioscorides' name for garlic—*Scorodon*. It can be grown in a wide variety of climates and day lengths if given a long enough growing season. Rocambole is a poor keeper.

Few nurseries offer this plant by its botanical name, so look for "top-setting" in descriptions. The greenish cloves are enclosed in purplish sheathing, but the best identifying characteristic is the twisting scapes topped by bulbils. These bulbils are offered in many nursery catalogs as "rocambole seeds." True seed is seldom produced by the plant.

Garlic Strains with Limited Distribution or Common Names

Buon Gusto: Probably just another California Early or Late variety, this is the name given by Safeway stores to some of the garlic they carry. Safeway Buon Gusto took third prize at the Chez Panisse, Berkeley, garlic tasting on July 14, 1981.

Elephant garlic: Elephant garlic is not a variety of garlic, despite what some nurseries would have you believe. It is a separate species of *Allium* with a distinct, but mild, garlic flavor.

Silverskin: Silverskin is a common name given to many strains of garlic with white sheathing. This is the basic white garlic offered by many nurseries. Most claim that theirs is "unique" or the "best so far."

Spanish Rojo: A pungent red garlic variety that originated in Spain. Very drought-tolerant, it can be dry-farmed without irrigation. It is almost impossible to find the true Spanish Rojo in the United States.

Susanville garlic: A strain with small firm white bulbs and large cloves. Introduced by S & H Organic Acres in 1982.

Miscellaneous varieties: Garlic varieties bearing the common names red, German red, early red, dago red, blue, Greek blue, and blue Italian are probably all originally derived from one of the twenty or so Spanish Rojo, South American, or Chilean types.

Wild garlic: Too many plants throughout the world have been given the common name *wild garlic* to be able to sort out which is which. Most are not clove-forming, and many are more like onions than garlic. *Allium canadense*, known as wild garlic, meadow leek, rose leek, and wild onion, is one such bulb. It is native to North America.

In Forks of Salmon, near the Oregon/California border, LSR members have cultivated garlic which is braided with dried flowers and marketed under this label.

To grow garlic successfully, bear these facts in mind.

1. Most garlic crops are fall-planted in mild-winter areas. In California, the expert growers in Gilroy, Hollister, and Salinas may plant specially selected varieties as late as March, but home growers should stick to a fall planting schedule.

2. Climate and latitude are important considerations in selecting a variety of garlic to plant because garlic is extremely sensitive to seasonal change.

3. The most important feature of the changing seasons to a garlic plant is the lengthening of days as spring approaches and turns to summer. Warm temperatures speed the processes of maturity and bulb formation, but it is actually the long days that signal the plants to form bulbs.

4. Garlic is usually harvested in July or August in the northern hemisphere. Summer rainfall as the bulb is maturing or before harvest can rot the bulb's sheathing.

5. Many nurseries and seed companies ship for fall planting only, so orders must be placed by late summer. Unfortunately, most suppliers do not offer named cultivar varieties for sale. They ship the 'Early' variety because it will produce bulbs in adverse conditions.

6. While dormant, the bulbs *must* be stored in unheated conditions. If they are exposed to cold temperatures around 40°F (6°C) for one to nine months in storage, bulbs will quickly and vigorously begin to develop after planting.

7. Cloves, not seeds, are planted, although agriculturalists often refer to the cloves as "seed" or planting stock.

8. To prevent cloves from drying out, they are not separated from the bulbs until it is time to plant.

9. If growing plants are not exposed to temperatures below 60°F (20°C), they often fail to form bulbs. This is another reason for fall planting. Winter temperatures usually satisfy the requirement.

10. Garlic is a "heavy feeder." This means that it needs lots of nitrogen during its growing season (but not during the bulb-formation period).

How to Grow Garlic

Most people plant everything in spring out of habit, but your chances of producing lovely, large garlic bulbs are slim if you follow a spring planting schedule. Garlic growing is easy when you plant in fall. Take some time before you plant to select a proper site and examine the soil. Full sun is best for a garlic patch, but if you can't find a spot that receives sunlight all day, be sure to find one that receives *at least* 6 hours and hope for the best. Try to avoid windy locations and low spots that are cold pockets or drainage collection points. If you can, select a variety adapted to your climate.

Soil quality is just as important as sunlight. Ideals have been established based on the fact that good drainage and an abundance of organic matter are essential. Skipping the ideals, let it be said that rich alluvial soils or sandy loams with slightly acid to neutral pH are preferred. Improve your soil if it fails to meet these criteria. Remove weeds. It is best to plant in a soil that has not been planted the previous year with either garlic or onions. If your situation is hopeless, i.e., clay soil that will not drain or rocky/alkaline conditions, build a raised bed and add potting mix, creating what is basically just a big container.

Sets: Curious as it may seem, nurseries that sell garlic "sets" actually just provide heads of garlic. In horticultural jargon *sets* refers to small propagative parts. Onion sets are small bulblets, but in garlic terms, sets are cloves. Even though garlic purchased at the supermarket can be planted, your chances for success are better if you use planting stock from a nursery or from stock saved and properly stored from a previous harvest. Even though bulbs sold for planting stock are edible, be aware that they may have been treated to control mites.

Transplants: Some nurseries ship tiny plants of garlic and garlic relatives in small pots of soil. The value of these transplants is that they can be spring planted. This is useful if you neglected to plant in fall or if your fall planting failed. Some growers in extremely cold winter areas have better luck with transplants. Nursery transplants are expensive. You can raise transplants yourself indoors or in a cold frame using sets in fall. Handle all transplants carefully. The roots should not be damaged. Plant as soon as the soil can be worked in spring and then follow normal growing procedures.

Planting: Water the soil thoroughly and firm it before planting. The cloves that constitute the planting stock should not be separated from the heads until they are ready to go into the ground. Do not peel them. Many believe that the slender cloves from the center of the head make poor planting stock. The blunt end of a clove is the root end. Place cloves pointed end up in small, 1- to 2-inch- (2.5- to 5-centimeter-) deep holes spaced about 4 inches (10 cm) apart in the prepared soil and cover loosely. If you are planting in rows, space them from 1 to 2 feet (30 to 60 cm) apart.

Fertilize with a high-nitrogen organic or commercial fertilizer at the time of planting. Well-composted soils will usually have plenty of nutrients. Phosphorus is one of the three essential nutrients, but most soils or fertilizers provide necessary amounts. There is a myth that bone meal, which supplies phosphorus, is the best thing you can feed garlic. It certainly won't hurt, but if plants do not receive nitrogen when they are actively growing, the bulbs will not be voluptuous. Too much nitrogen, however, is undesirable. Do not fertilize in summer.

Covering the planting area with a mulch helps keep down weeds, retain soil moisture, and protect bulbs from freezing and roots from freeze/thaw heaving.

Never plant sickly looking or soft cloves, and do *not* set out transplants (if that is your method) that exhibit signs of disease. If you infest the soil, you can ruin your whole crop and make it impossible to plant any alliums in the soil for years to come.

In most parts of the United States, plant sets between September 15 and October 15. South of the Mason-Dixon Line, plant as late as November 1. Plant any time from fall to early winter in mild-winter areas of California, Texas, and Louisiana.

Cold-winter areas: Those who live in climates where winter temperatures are severe may choose any of three methods and times for planting. Fox Hill Farm in Michigan has good results planting sets in mid- to late summer after other vegetables have been harvested and the soil has been re-prepared. Richters in Canada recommends fall planting. Traditionally, people in cold climates start transplants in fall or winter from sets. These are planted outdoors in spring just as soon as the ground can be worked. But garlic can be grown from sets in fall in Alaska if it is mulched enough to prevent the bulbs from freezing.

Growth: Growth begins immediately after the cloves have been planted, so keep the soil moist (not soggy-wet). Watering deeply about once a week is usually sufficient if rainfall doesn't do the job. Roots develop first, and they need about a month to develop before the first hard frost. If you neglected to mulch, throw plastic sheeting or old blankets or shower curtains over the planting area the night frost is expected.

These bulbs are shallow-rooted, so weeds offer stiff competition for nutrients and moisture in the upper 2 feet (60 cm) of soil. Shoots do not appear until several weeks or months after planting. Snow or a hard frost may kill the shoots, but the bulbs are still alive, and they will send up new shoots in spring. Fertilize a second time in spring. Keep the soil free of weeds. Never permit the soil to dry out completely or the developing cloves may sprout when the soil is newly moistened.

As the weather warms and days grow longer, plants mature. The more top growth that occurs before the bulbs enlarge, the better the yield. *Do* pinch off any flower heads that may appear. Energy is directed from bulbs to flower heads, and bulbs will be stunted if flowers are allowed to develop. (Many garlic cultivars do not flower.) Stop watering about a month before harvest.

Reasons for failure: If plants have not had sufficient time to develop, they will be immature when it is time to harvest. Immature garlic is stunted, small, or shriveled. If bulbs don't develop properly the problem could also be a simple matter of latitude or climate. Either you are growing a variety not suited to the day length and temperature in your garden, or you didn't plant in fall. Short day length in low (i.e., subtropical or tropical) latitudes can be a real problem; try planting in summer.

Of course, there may be many other reasons for failure. Rough-looking bulbs can be the product of a heavy clay soil, or overly vigorous growth due to wide spacing, too-early planting, or overfertilizing. Irrigation or rainfall toward the end of the growing season is usually to blame for rotted sheathing or blackened bulbs.

Organic gardeners love to grow garlic because it keeps insects away from their kitchen vegetables and herbs. Garlic is not prone to problems, but some beasties think it is a delicious treat—and who can blame them? Stem and bulb nematodes are probably the cause when problems occur. Nematodes are difficult to eradicate from the soil once they are established, so do not plant in soil where garlic or onions have suffered in the past. Onion thrips, Japanese onion aphids, onion maggots, wireworms, and several kinds of mites can also hamper your efforts to grow garlic, and like most bulbs, garlic is susceptible to fungus diseases. If you plant healthy stock in a soil that drains easily, your chances for success are quite good.

Note: Because most bulbs are susceptible to fungus diseases, many countries have regulations to protect their crops from infestations. Alliums usually cannot be shipped from one country to another without special permits.

How to Grow and Harvest Rocambole

Most of the remarks above about growing garlic also apply to rocambole, but this plant is not as fussy about day length: it can be grown successfully from Canada to Los Angeles if given a long-enough growing season. It can grow in fairly heavy, clayey soils. Do not remove the flower stalks if you want bulbils to form.

Late summer or early fall planting is best for cloves. Treat them just like garlic and harvest the following summer when the tops turn brown. Leave the bulbils on the tops during drying and curing. The tops are not very pliable, and braiding can be difficult. Tie or braid and hang in a dark and cool, but dry and airy, place.

CARYL SAUNDERS ASSOCIATES

The unsung heroes of the
Garlic Revolution are the
workers who harvest the
garlic, making our pleasure
possible. Thanks to all of
them from Lovers of the
Stinking Rose.

Plant bulbils ½ inch deep in fall in mild-winter climates or in early spring where winters are severe. Their young shoots look like grass and take about two years to produce full-size bulbs. By the end of the first summer, the plants look like scallions and taste like garlic. Leave them in the ground through the fall and winter. By the end of the second summer, both underground bulbs and bulbils topping the flower stalks will have formed. Harvest, dry, and cure, then store.

Harvest, Curing, and Storage

"Fresh garlic" is a bit of a misnomer. Garlic pulled straight from the earth can be eaten, but its delightful pungent flavor fully emerges in the drying and curing process that removes excess moisture. Garlic flavor is at its peak when this process is completed—about one month after harvest. This is when garlic is termed "fresh."

Curing ensures that the bulbs will keep well. If they are not thoroughly dry at their centers, they mold in storage. Curing also helps prevent bruising. Garlic keeps for months if properly stored, but flavor deteriorates as time goes by.

Braided or tied in bunches in a cool, well-ventilated place out of sunlight, some garlic varieties will last for up to a year. Different varieties have different keeping qualities—a "good keeper" is one that will be firm and delicious long after it is harvested. A "poor keeper" will only last a few months before it begins to soften.

Garlic is pretty braided, but it can also be stored in mesh onion bags, in old nylon stockings, or on wire racks. As long as it is dried thoroughly and then placed where air can circulate freely around it, it should be fine. Garages and basements may offer ideal storage conditions, but if temperatures hover around 40°F (4° to 5°C), the cloves often sprout. Other methods for storing garlic include dehydrating, puréeing and storing in the refrigerator, and marinating in vegetable or olive oil and storing in the refrigerator.

Large-scale agriculture: Garlic is harvested by hand by workers who pull up the bulbs and windrow them for curing. The garlic tops act as their own thatch, protecting the bulbs in the windrows from sunburn and from dew or fog. When rain threatens, the bulbs must be moved to sheds. Rain rarely threatens in California in late summer, one reason it is a prime garlic-growing area.

Both roots and tops are usually left on bulbs until drying is complete—after one or two weeks. Then roots and tops are removed by hand, and the bulbs are either field-cured under the protection of their tops, or they are sacked up in onion bags and placed in bins to cure. The old dry tops and roots are not rototilled back into the soil because they can infect it with the various beasties mentioned in the horticultural discussion (above). Mechanized harvesting is only used for bulbs that will be processed into the many products that contain dehydrated or puréed garlic.

Kitchen gardening: Harvest time for the home gardener is July or August (in the northern hemisphere), but it varies with the climate and variety planted. Some people advocate harvesting as soon as the tops begin turning yellow. Others say wait until the tops bend over and die. Pull or dig up a few sample bulbs the moment the first tops yellow to check development. If cloves are well formed and beginning to separate, your crop is ripe for harvesting.

Heavy rainfall or irrigation around harvest time can cause the bulbs to rot. Dig them up immediately if the soil becomes saturated with water, and get them under cover to dry. Never let the roots get wet, or even moist, once they have been harvested because they may begin to grow. Discard any diseased or damaged bulbs. Dry thoroughly for about two weeks in the shade of a tree or building or in a shed, garage, or closet.

Curing follows the initial drying period. Trim the roots off with shears at this time, leaving about ½ inch of root. Then braid the bulbs, or simply bunch them together by their tops and hang them from rafters or herb drying stands. Or, cut off the tops about an inch from the heads and cure on racks, in slatted bins, or in mesh bags.

Stored at 70 percent or more humidity, garlic quickly molds and often sprouts roots. Do not refrigerate whole garlic bulbs. After about a week to a month of curing, they are ready to eat, dehydrate, purée, or marinate.

To purée: Peel and quickly whirl in a food processor or blender. Put the purée in jars with either a teaspoon of lemon juice per ½ pint or enough olive oil to give a nice consistency. This purée can be refrigerated immediately, or you can let the jars ferment for a few days before refrigerating. Mix with olive oil if you choose to ferment. Refrigerate for at least a day before you open the jar.

To dehydrate: Slice in ⅛-inch slices. (Elephant garlic slices easily with a potato peeler.) Sun-dry the slices under cheesecloth or place in a dehydrator or gas oven. When the slices turn to chips that snap, they can be stored in a tightly sealed jar and kept for years in a cool cupboard. Do not refrigerate chips. Pop them in your mouth for snacks, or toss them in salads, soups, and sauces.

To marinate: Slice and place in a jar of extra-virgin olive oil in the refrigerator. Add herbs to the marinade if desired. Lesser grades of olive oil will congeal under refrigeration.

ACKNOWLEDGMENTS: Walter Doty, Horticulturalist; Joe Gubser, Joseph Gubser Co.; Marilyn Hampstead, Fox Hill Farm; Jack Kakis, Monterey Agricultural Products; Paul and Charlene Lee, The Platonic Academy of the Herb Renaissance; Michael MacCaskey, Horticulturalist; Alice Rogers; F. F. "Cal" Slewing, S & H Organic Acres; Ronald E. Voss, Extension Vegetable Specialist; Lance Walheim, Horticulturalist; and the American Institute of Wine and Food.

Garlic Source Calendar

Fresh garlic is available throughout the year because it is grown and harvested in different parts of the world. Generally, the garlic-growing regions of the United States—such as California and Louisiana—supply most of our needs, but certain months of the year would be barren of garlic if it were not for shipments from Mexico and other countries.

Here's a calendar prepared by Gilroy Farms, one of the largest garlic growers in California.

January: Early White from Argentina
February: Creole (pink) and Egyptian (white) from Mexico
March: Early White from Chile
April: Chileano (pink) from Mexico
May: Early White from Mexico
June: California Early (white)
July through December: California Late (white)

(See pages 30-33 for descriptions of each of these varieties.)

The onion family is quickly subdued by cooking. Not only are its odor compounds driven off by high temperatures, but some of them appear to be converted into another complex molecule that is 50 to 70 times sweeter than a molecule of table sugar.

Harold McGee
On Food and Cooking *(Scribner's)*

There's no doubt that after you eat a lot of garlic, you just kind of feel like you are floating, you feel ultra-confident, you feel capable of going out and whipping your weight in wild cats. . . .
It's not like being drunk. Being drunk is a different kind of euphoria. Being stoned is a different kind of euphoria. Garlic euphoria is kind of like you've got both feet planted on the ground—you're a part of the world. You are not, you know, apart from it. And yet, you definitely do feel real good.

Michael Goodwin in
Garlic Is as Good as Ten Mothers
by Les Blank

III

GARLIC

The Food

*A GARLIC COOKBOOK can no longer be simply a lot of recipes with twice the
amount of garlic (or more) as is usually called for in such dishes. An extra garlicky
lasagne or frittata is not really of much interest to a bona fide lover of the stinking
rose. Anyone can double or quadruple the amount of garlic in a recipe to suit his or
her craving. There are many garlic cookbooks now on the market (see Garlic Bibliography), and they have between them hundreds of garlicky recipes. So the world
really doesn't need another garlic-recipe collection.*

*However, what the serious garlic lover might well appreciate is a small collection
of all-garlic menus—combinations of garlicky recipes that go well together, creating
a veritable garlic festival in one's own home. This is what* The Official Garlic Lovers
Handbook *provides—garlic menus, some ethnic in orientation, others eclectic or seasonal, made up of tested recipes collected from professional chefs, restaurateurs, cooking teachers, and the membership of Lovers of the Stinking Rose. (Additional recipes
are included in two interesting essays at the end of this section.)*

*Another common characteristic of garlic cookbooks is instructions that tell all
about mincing and puréeing garlic, how to bake whole heads of garlic, how to store
garlic, and how to get the odor of garlic off of the breath and hands.* The Official
Garlic Lovers Handbook *assumes that the reader has a working knowledge of cooking with fresh garlic. You may wish to consult other garlic cookbooks for basic cooking
and preparation techniques for garlic, but our job here is to stimulate your taste buds
with orchestrated garlic menus, as well as some in-depth exploration of garlic themes
and variations.*

*There are a few rules of thumb that pertain to cooking with garlic that I will
review here, because they summarize the essential characteristics of garlic:*

Cal Swiss Garlic is the name of a California garlic packer. We like their public-relations approach!

≈ *Garlic Rule No. 1: When preparing garlic for cooking, the more you do to it, the more it will do to you. In its raw state, the more you break down the garlic's cell walls, releasing the volatile sulphur-containing oils, the more severe will be the chemical reactions that create the sharp (burning) taste of garlic. So, using a garlic press* creates the sharpest-tasting garlic, and chopping garlic coarsely with a knife produces a less sharp- but still raw-tasting garlic. Food processors are slightly less violent than garlic presses.*

---

* *To press or not to press, that is the question. I have over a dozen garlic presses, including one that has been designed and produced by an LSR member. It is called "The Garlic Squeeze" and retails for over $30. Could it be "wrong" to use these devices? Some food professionals say "Yes." Sue Kreitzman, in her wonderful book, Garlic, says of garlic presses, "They will reduce garlic to an evil-smelling mush."*

It is true that garlic's subtle potentials are lost through the violence of the garlic press. Yet, there are times when I enjoy that sharp "evil-smelling mush." I might add that the better garlic presses have larger holes, which create a kind of mince/purée, and the flavor is not so harsh.

≈ *Garlic Rule No. 2: When cooking garlic, the more you do to it, the less it will do to you. The longer the cooking time, the milder the flavor of garlic, because prolonged exposure to heat denatures the chemicals that create garlic's strong flavor. Forty-Clove Chicken, the recipe that James Beard popularized in the 1960s, was a surprise to people who equated quantity of garlic with strength of garlic. The 40-clove dish renders the garlic mild and nutty from prolonged cooking.*

≈ *Garlic Rule No. 3: Burning garlic cancels Garlic Rule No. 2. Long moderate heat renders the garlic mild. Hot direct heat—such as frying—can burn the garlic, producing an acrid or pungent flavor that is not terribly desirable. I say this in a qualified way because there are always exceptions to rules, and then exceptions to the exceptions.*

Case in point: I have had a Spanish Gypsy dish called Coliflora Gitano (see Garlic Times, Issue #12, for the recipe), where the accidentally burned garlic was mashed into cauliflower with lots of olive oil. Delicious! And, the popularity of garlic bagels, at least in California, goes against all the rules. Garlic bagels are crusted with dehydrated garlic flakes—oh no!—and then, when you toast the bagel, the garlic burns—oh my god! But spread with good-quality cream cheese, this garlic travesty is transformed into a great treat.

So much for rules.

So, to summarize the basic rules, you can create more of garlic's potent flavor with one clove of garlic pressed into a dish at the last minute before serving than you can by adding 40 cloves of garlic at the beginning of a long-cooking stew or roast.

The Taste of Garlic

≈ L. JOHN HARRIS ≈

IN THIS TIME of chic food, it is increasingly common to taste foods and beverages not only for pleasure or hunger, but also for the experience of subtle variations in flavor, texture, etc. Food professionals often conduct food tastings, where, in a format similar to wine tastings, they sample foods and products as diverse as olive oils and chocolate candies.

Often, manufacturers and suppliers of these foodstuffs participate in tastings at department stores and specialty shops to introduce items to the consumer. Using this approach with garlic inevitably produces interesting and somewhat funny results.

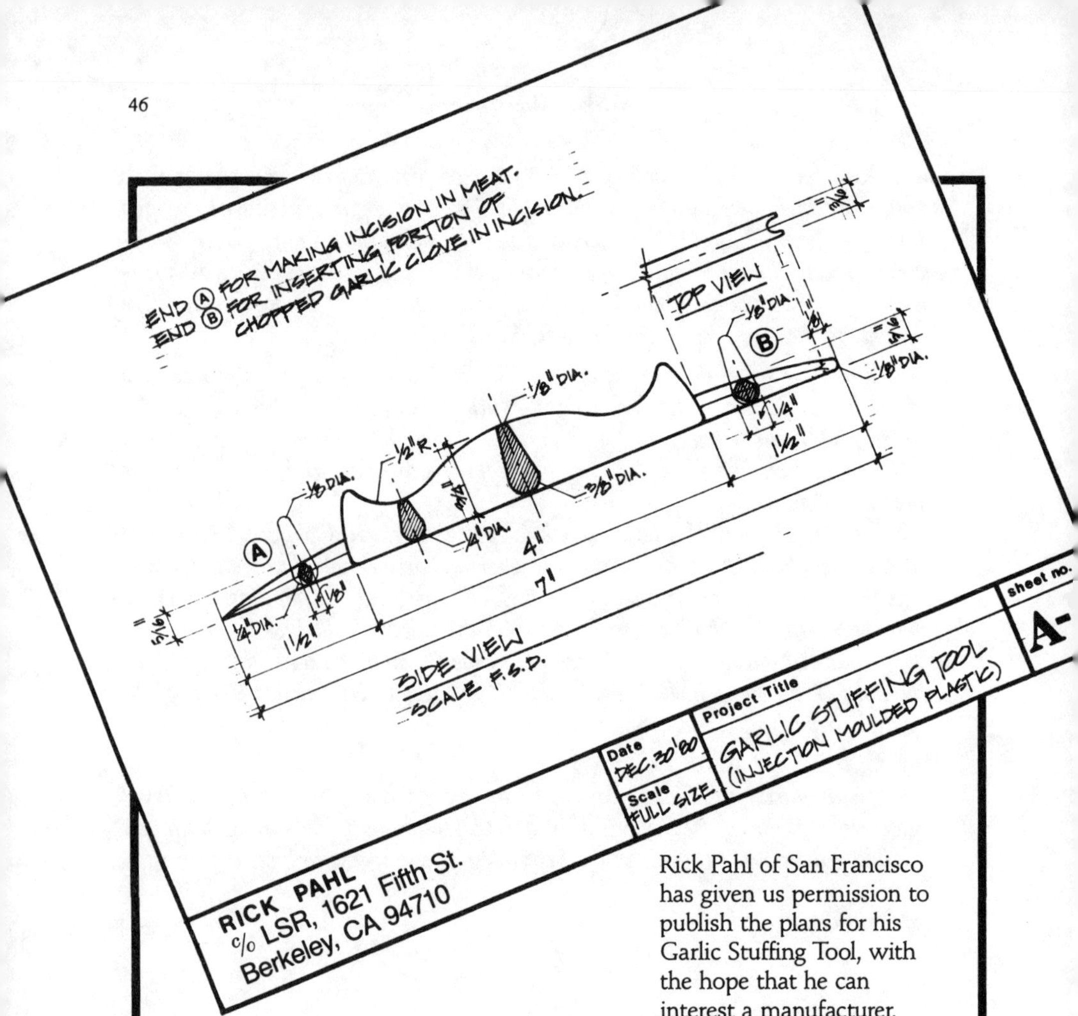

END Ⓐ FOR MAKING INCISION IN MEAT.
END Ⓑ FOR INSERTING PORTION OF
CHOPPED GARLIC CLOVE IN INCISION.

TOP VIEW

⅛"DIA.

Ⓑ

⅛"DIA.

⅛"DIA.

1"/4

1½"

⅛"DIA.

½"R.

⅜"DIA.

⅛"DIA.

¼"DIA.

4"

Ⓐ

¼"DIA.

1½"

7"

SIDE VIEW
SCALE F.S.D.

sheet no.
A-

Date
DEC. 30' 80

Project Title
GARLIC STUFFING TOOL
(INJECTION MOULDED PLASTIC)

Scale
FULL SIZE

RICK PAHL
c/o LSR, 1621 Fifth St.
Berkeley, CA 94710

Rick Pahl of San Francisco has given us permission to publish the plans for his Garlic Stuffing Tool, with the hope that he can interest a manufacturer. When garlic slivers are to be inserted in meat or poultry, one end of the device makes an incision and the other, blunt end pushes the sliver in.

In 1981, at Chez Panisse restaurant in Berkeley, California, a garlic tasting was organized by co-owner and host, Jerry Budrick. Eight varieties and strains of garlic were sampled. At a large table, a number of curious and bemused chefs, food writers, and garlic aficionados sat with cloves from the various sample bulbs, marked numerically. Each tester had a form with which to rate the numbered garlics.

Terms such as *pungent, sharp, sweet, juicy, nutty, bouquet, bitter,* and *bland* were used with great gusto.

Actually, the event was informative, even if amusing and somewhat pretentious in its formal treatment of this humble bulb. The problems with any such tasting are those of subjectivity and the use of language. What is the difference between *potent, pungent,* and *sharp*? What does *sweet* really mean when applied to garlic? And how do you quantify *juicy*?

Semantic problems aside, you can, without being an expert or a snob, discern differences among various garlics. The qualities of most available garlics are readily apparent. Alice Waters and Thérèse Shere wrote in *Cook's Magazine* (September/October, 1985) that:

> Garlic varies considerably in flavor and quality depending on where it is grown, how it is cured, and how long it is kept after harvest. At harvest in early summer, and for a short time afterwards, garlic's flavor is at its most delicate. This is the time to use it uncooked in the classic aïoli, rouille, pesto, quickly sautéed, or gently stewed. As garlic ages, the flavor becomes sharper and more lingering, and the garlic is better cooked more thoroughly—baked whole, the purée eaten with rough bread, added to vegetable purées, or served with roasted potatoes or grilled chicken. Immature garlic is delicious too, harvested when the bulb just begins to swell—bigger than a scallion, but before the separate cloves begin to form.

As for the flavor of the basic white garlic from California, the early-harvested version is not as strong as the late variety. More potent still is a variety called Spanish Rojo (also known as rojas), which is not all that common, but which may be the ancestor of the more popular reddish-colored garlics, Creole and Chileno. These dark-colored garlics with strong flavor are sometimes referred to as Italian, but should not be confused with a cultivar known as *Allium sativum* "Italian," which is grown along with Creole in Louisiana. The Italian variety is even more potent than the Creole. The Mexican garlic we get in the stores early in the year is described by Alice Waters as spicy but without a lingering taste. (Talk about a developed palate!) This purple-reddish garlic with small cloves is related to the other red garlics described above.

You can see that there are many nuances for the average consumer to be aware of when it comes to purchasing and tasting garlic. True lovers of the stinking rose may want to pursue the development of their garlic palates and their "taste memory," as one chef describes it. Others, and I include myself to some degree, may be satisfied with the notion that all truly fresh garlic—firm, heavy bulbs with no sprouting visible at the top of the stem end, and no strong smells when put to the nose (which would indicate that sprouting had begun, although not visibly)—can be enjoyed without a lot of "tasting." For no matter how different Spanish Rojo may be from California Early, the differences cannot compare to, nor matter as much as, the differences between wines, or even olive oils for that matter.

Which is not to knock the professional tasters. We need their savvy to keep us well informed, and to keep honest the people that supply us with the products we purchase.

The Cesnaka Garlic Rating Scale

Here is a reproduction of the garlic grading scale created by Jerry Budrick for Chez Panisse's garlic tasting, held on July 14, 1981. Jerry's *cesnaka* (the Czech word for garlic) scale is the first known system for evaluating garlic's subtle flavor and handling nuances.

```
          The First Garlic Tasting- Bastille Day, July 14, 1981

A tasting of various garlics at Chez Panisse, Berkeley

Name of taster_____ Number of tasters_____

The garlics will be ranked according to tasters' preferences, not
     necessarily by points as determined by the following:

     Cesnaka Garlic Rating Scale- 37 Points Maximum

1. Whole head
        a. General appearance (aesthetics: color, shape, tightness,
             vibrancy) -1 - +1
        b. Picker's treatment (whiskers, stalk, residual dirt) -1 -+1
        c. Texture (flaccidity, resiliency, hollowness, turbidity) -1 -+1
        d. Ease of separation 0 -+1
        e. Number and size of cloves -1 - +1
        f. Ratio of garlic to skin -1 -+1

2. Unpeeled clove
        a. Color 0 -+1
        b. Texture (mushiness, firmness) -1 -+2
        c. Peelability (subjective according to profession) 0 -+2

3. Peeled clove
        a. Transparency of peel 0 -+1
        b. Stickiness (to fingers, knives, under nails) -1 - 0
        c. Fragrance -1 - +1
        d. Rot or blemishes -2 - 0
        e. Snappability (crispness) 0 -+1
        f. Texture 0 -+1

4. Sliced or broken clove
        a. Inner beauty -1 -+2
        b. Aroma -1 -+3
        c. Dessication or juiciness -1 -+3

5. Baked whole heads of garlic
        a. General appearance -1 -+1
        b. Texture 0 -+1
        c. Fragrance 0 -+2
        d. Savour 0 -+4

6. Raw peeled cloves in tasting
        a. Heat -2 -+1
        b. Flavor 0 -+4
        c. Balance -1 -+1

There will be sangria served before, during and after the tasting for
     cleansing the palate.  Foods provided will be peasant bread and
     butter, tomato and onion salad with garlic-free vinaigrette, and
     corn on the cob with garlic-free butter
```

Says Jerry of the event: "After lengthy discussion concerning the proper method of tasting garlic, the panel settled into a quite serious evaluation of the various garlics. All aspects of the species were considered, beginning with the whole head in a raw state, continuing through the clove, unpeeled and peeled, culminating with the head and clove baked à la Alice Waters."

The Chez Panisse Garlic Festival

Tuesday
July 12
$10.00

Garlic cooked inside a brioche pastry
Fresh vegetable ragoût with basil and garlic
Richard Olney's baked lamb shank dish cooked with garlic
and white wine
Fresh fruits

Wednesday
July 13
$10.00

Salad with mushrooms, avocado, various lettuces,
julienne of carrots, and tomatoes with fresh herbs and
garlic dressing and chapons
Special Catalan recipe for garlic sausage served with new
potatoes
Roast chicken with garlic and olive oil, served with puréed
garlic spread on the chicken
Fresh fruits

Thursday
July 14
$20.00

Bastille Day with The Louisiana Playboys: Live Cajun Music
Whole baked garlic heads served with peasant breads
and white cheese with green onions
Provençal vegetable soup with a liaison of fresh basil & garlic
Brochettes of fresh fish grilled with whole garlics and branches
of thyme
Barons of lamb charcoal-roasted, served with a gratin of
eggplant
Figs cooked with garlic, honey, and red wine

Friday
July 15
$20.00

Bagna cauda — warm anchovy, garlic, and cream bath
served with an array of fresh vegetables
Fresh pasta served with a herb sauce of pounded basil, sorrel,
garlic, burnet, hyssop, roquette and olive oil
Fish ragoût cooked with onions, garlic, tomatoes, and fish
fumet
Recipe of Troisgros — pigeons stuffed with whole garlic and
roasted
Fresh fruits

Saturday
July 16
$20.00

Garlic Hors d'oeuvre: Roasted peppers
Eggplant caviar
Garlic pickled eggs
Marinated mushrooms with garlic and bay
Green beans and carrots julienne with aïoli
Cucumber salad with crème fraîche and garlic
Fish Course: Steamed soft shell clams with garlic mayonnaise
The Garlic Entrée: Roast suckling pig from garlic fed sows
from the Dal Porto ranch in Amador County
Fresh fruits

Dedicated to Lovers of the Stinking Rose

Family-style dinners/two seatings/half bottle of Chez Panisse Zinfandel included

Menus and Recipes

THE FOLLOWING *recipes have been grouped into menus. Some of the menus are ethnic or are identified with one specific cuisine. Others are thematic: a menu for Thanksgiving, Christmas, and so on. All the menus are, we think, delicious and sufficiently garlicky to satisfy the most radical of garlic lovers. However, since amounts of garlic in any recipe are subjective, and can be affected by the kind of garlic being used, we ask that the cook evaluate the particular situation and adjust the amounts of garlic accordingly.*

Many of the menus could benefit from a green salad, rice, a vegetable, or some other side dish. We have provided only the primary, garlicky courses.

All recipes serve from 4 to 6 people unless otherwise noted.

Bastille Day Garlic Festival Menu
≈ CHEZ PANISSE ≈

ON JULY 14, 1976, Chez Panisse restaurant held the first known garlic festival in America. LSR provided the inspiration for the event and a garlic-honey topping for ice cream. Chez Panisse provided the following menu that proved to be the model for garlic meals and festivals throughout America. From this menu we have selected four of the recipes (in the form that they were given to LSR) that were first published in the inaugural issue of Garlic Times (Spring, 1977).

Champignons à l'ail aux feuilles des vignes
(Whole Garlics and Mushrooms)

Purée d'ail rôti, cuisse de poulet
(Baked Chicken Legs with Garlic Purée)

Aïoli aux haricots verts et pommes de terre
(Green Beans and Potatoes with Aïoli)

Nouilles fraîches, sauce pistou
(Pasta with Garlic, Basil, and Olive Oil)

Tripes au pistou
(Beef Tripe with Basil and Garlic)

Bourride
(Poached Fish in Fish Stock with Aïoli)

Gigot rôti
(Roast Leg of Lamb Marinated and Stuffed with Garlic)

Purée de pommes de terre à l'ail
(Puréed Potatoes and Garlic-Infused Cream)

Garlic Ice Cream Sunday

Whole Garlics and Mushrooms

Sauté 15 whole mushrooms and 15 whole peeled garlic cloves in 1 cup olive oil until slightly tender. Sprinkle with salt and pepper to taste, and a pinch of thyme and marjoram.

Lay a bed of grape leaves in a baking pan and place mushrooms and garlics on top. Lay another layer of grape leaves on top and drizzle with olive oil.

Bake for 30 minutes at 350° or until mushrooms and garlics are very soft.

Serve warm in individual dishes, circling the mushrooms and garlics with the grape leaves.

Baked Chicken Legs with Garlic Purée

Rub four leg/thigh chicken pieces with olive oil, salt, and pepper.

Place on a bed of sliced peeled garlic—about 20 cloves—coated in olive oil in a baking pan.

Bake skin-side down at 350° until pieces are brown, then turn over and continue baking until skin side is brown.

Remove chicken pieces and press garlic through a sieve or food mill, pouring off excess olive oil. Spread this purée over chicken pieces and serve.

Roast Leg of Lamb Marinated and Stuffed with Garlic

Marinade: Mix 1 cup of red wine, 1 cup chopped garlic, and 1 cup diced carrots, onions, etc. with 1 cup olive oil. Set aside.

Stuffing for lamb: Make from 1- to 2-inch-deep slits in lamb with a sharp, narrow knife blade. Insert slivers of garlic first, then strips of prosciutto.

Rub lamb with marinade and place, covered, in refrigerator overnight. (Make sure lamb is smothered in the marinade.)

Roast lamb according to any standard recipe and serve with the following dish.

Puréed Potatoes and Garlic-Infused Cream

Make mashed potatoes according to any standard recipe, but keep them on the dry side by reducing the recipe's liquid.

Simmer about 6 peeled cloves of garlic in about 1 cup cream until garlic is soft.

Press garlic through a sieve into the potatoes along with the cream. Add salt and pepper to taste.

Hardcore Summer Menu

Bloody Miracles

Hardcore Garlic Salad

Garlic and Chili Grilled Shrimp Sandwiches

Garlic Ice Cream

SEVERAL of the most garlicky recipes have been grouped in this menu. It would make a great hot weather, outdoor lunch. It makes us think of Mexico or the Caribbean.

Bloody Miracles
≈ L. JOHN HARRIS ≈

This is a refreshing and healthful tonic which satisfies the requirements of many health practitioners. It has fiber (celery), garlic (raw, for maximum cardiovascular effect), and alchohol, which some experts claim is beneficial in small amounts to the cardiovascular system. The Tabasco sauce may also have beneficial qualities, and the lemon juice has vitamin C. Commercial tomato juice has too much salt, but it has vitamins and probably some fiber.

Vodka
Tomato juice
1 clove garlic, crushed, per serving
Tabasco sauce to taste

Lemon juice to taste
Herbs such as cilantro, dill, or basil,
   for garnish
1 stalk celery, for garnish

The ratio of vodka to tomato juice is up to you, but experts say to limit alcohol consumption to 2 ounces a day for maximum health benefits. A good ratio per serving would be about 2 ounces vodka to 6 ounces tomato juice.

Combine vodka, tomato juice, garlic, Tabasco sauce, and lemon juice. Mix well. Garnish with herbs and celery.

Hardcore Garlic Salad
≈ BRUCE AIDELLS ≈

Bruce has been an active LSR member and contributed recipes to The Book of Garlic. *His sausages, sold under the label of Aidells Sausage Company, are some of the best in the country, and they are used by top restaurants.*

1 red bell pepper
1 green bell pepper
Garlic cloves from 6 heads, peeled
1 teaspoon salt
4 tablespoons good fruity olive oil
3 tablespoons red wine vinegar

½ cup chopped parsley
2 tablespoons chopped fresh herbs
   of choice (e.g., basil, oregano,
   savory, marjoram), or 1
   tablespoon dried herbs of choice
Salt and pepper to taste

Char-roast peppers over flame, then steam in paper bag 15 minutes. Peel under water; drain and slice into thin strips. Blanch garlic cloves in 2 quarts boiling salted water for 4 minutes; then immerse in cold water. Place all vegetables in a bowl and combine. Mix together oil, vinegar, parsley, and herbs, adding salt and pepper to taste. Pour over salad, tossing to coat thoroughly.

Garlic and Chili Grilled Shrimp Sandwiches

The marinade in this recipe comes from The American Bar & Grill in Los Angeles, a participant in the first Los Angeles Garlic Week. The aïoli (garlic mayonnaise) is basic and can be found in many cookbooks.

2 pounds large shrimp, shelled and
   deveined

Marinade:
4 onions, chopped
8 tablespoons butter (1 stick)
4 California dried chilies, ground
½ cup chili powder

Salt to taste
1 cup garlic cloves, peeled and
   pressed
2 cups olive oil

Sandwich makings:
French bread
Aïoli (see *The Book of Garlic*, page
   237, or variation below)

Lettuce
Red onion (optional)

Prepare marinade: Sauté onions in butter until soft. Add ground chilies and chili powder, and salt to taste. Let cool. Add pressed garlic and olive oil, and mix well. Marinate shrimp in mixture overnight.

When ready to make sandwiches, slice French bread and toast. Rub toast with a cut clove of garlic. Grill shrimp, about 1 to 2 minutes on each side. Make sandwiches from the toasted bread, aïoli, grilled shrimp, lettuce, and optional red onion.

Aïoli variation:

¼ of onion and garlic solids from
 marinade
2 tablespoons chopped garlic

3 egg yolks
2 tablespoons vinegar

After marinating the shrimp overnight, the leftover marinade can be incorporated when making the aïoli for an extra spicy sandwich.

Take the marinade solids and purée in a food processor with chopped garlic, egg yolks, and vinegar. Then add the marinade oil, just as you would in making a regular mayonnaise, until thick.

Garlic Ice Cream
≈ BARBARA FLASKA ≈

We are borrowing a recipe from The Book of Garlic *because it fits with this menu, and because it has been adopted by Nucleus Nuance restaurant in Los Angeles as their official garlic dessert. Nucleus Nuance started the first Los Angeles Garlic Week, and it served this ice cream to the local press. The recipe originated from Barbara Flaska, a member of LSR, and it was first published in* Garlic Times.

1 to 1½ teaspoons gelatin
¼ cup cold water
2 cups milk
¾ to 1 cup sugar

⅛ teaspoon salt
2 tablespoons lemon juice
2 cloves garlic, minced
2 cups whipping cream

Soak the gelatin in cold water. Bring the milk, sugar, and salt to a boil. Dissolve the gelatin in the hot milk. Cool, then add the lemon juice and garlic. Chill the mixture until slushy. Whip the cream until thick but not stiff and fold into the mixture. Freeze in a mold, or in a foil-covered tray.

Note: We have found that a fruit topping works well with this dessert.

Greek Menu

≈ MARTI SOUSANIS ≈

Lentil Soup

Lemon Garlic Chicken

Greek Potatoes

Beet Salad

MARTI GREW UP in a Greek-American family. She describes the following dishes as peasant dishes, but her culinary skills have refined them enormously. Marti is the author of The Art of Filo Cookbook *(Aris Books) and teaches cooking classes in the Bay Area and Michigan.*

Lentil Soup

This soup improves with age. I like eating it the next day, after the flavors have had a chance to mingle. The garnish was suggested by Aris' recipe testers, and I think it adds a nice, fresh punch to the soup.

1 lamb shank (or lamb bone)
10 cloves garlic (or 1 head), minced
4 onions, chopped medium
¼ cup olive oil
1 pound brown lentils
2½ quarts water
8 ounces tomato sauce
Large bunch of fresh parsley, finely chopped

1 teaspoon mustard seed
Salt and freshly ground pepper to taste
2 to 3 carrots, sliced

Garnish:
¼ cup finely chopped garlic
¼ cup finely chopped parsley
1 lemon, sliced

Brown the lamb shank or bone in the oven at 375° for approximately 20 minutes. Sauté the minced garlic and onions in olive oil until lightly browned.

Wash the lentils and drain. In a large, heavy pot mix together the lentils, water, tomato sauce, sautéed garlic and onions, and seasonings. Cover pot and bring to a boil. Simmer, stirring occasionally, for 1¾ hours. Add the carrots and simmer an additional 15 minutes. Remove the soup from heat. Take out the lamb shank and strip the meat from the bone. Chop the meat into small pieces and add to the soup.

To make the garnish, combine the garlic and parsley in a bowl.

Serve soup in bowls. Pass lemon slices and garnish separately.

Lemon Garlic Chicken

This may also be served with a rich rice pilaf, a simple fresh Greek salad, and the "infamous" retsina wine to create a Greek meal that everyone will enjoy.

1 whole chicken, cut up
10 cloves garlic (or 1 head), minced
4 tablespoons butter
2 large, juicy lemons
1 teaspoon dried, or 1 tablespoon
   fresh, oregano

Salt and freshly ground pepper to
   taste
Fresh parsley sprigs and lemon
   slices, for garnish

Preheat broiler. Place chicken in a large baking pan, skin-side down. Sprinkle half of the garlic on chicken and dot with half of the butter. Pour half the lemon juice over the ckicken. Add half of the oregano, and the salt and pepper. Broil on middle shelf of oven for 15 minutes, basting frequently.

Remove chicken from the oven. Turn the chicken pieces over. Distribute the remaining ingredients over the chicken and broil another 15 minutes, basting as it browns. If chicken starts to get too crisp, change the oven from broil to bake until the chicken is done.

Remove chicken from the oven. Pour the butter-lemon sauce from the pan over the chicken. Serve garnished with the parsley sprigs and lemon slices.

Greek Potatoes

This is my father's recipe. The trick is to get the potatoes crisp without burning the zucchini.

¾ cup olive oil
3 large potatoes, sliced ¼-inch
   thick
2 medium zucchini, sliced ¾-inch
   thick
6 to 8 cloves garlic, minced

2 cups whole tomatoes, peeled,
   including juice
½ teaspoon dried, or 1 tablespoon
   fresh, oregano
Salt and freshly ground pepper to
   taste

Pour ½ cup olive oil into a 10-by-16-inch baking pan. Place the potatoes in three rows in a single layer in the pan. Add the zucchini between the rows of potatoes. Sprinkle the garlic over the vegetables. Cut the tomatoes into small pieces and spread evenly over the potatoes and zucchini. Add the oregano, salt, and pepper. Sprinkle the remaining ¼ cup olive oil on top.

Bake in a 375° oven for 45 minutes or until the potatoes are crispy. Let them cool a little before serving.

Beet Salad

Beets are such an underrated vegetable in America, but they taste so good when marinated in this spicy dressing.

3 large fresh beets
3 large cloves garlic, finely minced
¼ cup fruity olive oil

Salt and freshly ground pepper to taste

Remove the beet tops. Wash the beets, place them in a pan, and cover with water. Bring to a boil. Lower flame and simmer until the beets are cooked (about 40 minutes, depending on the size). Remove from heat, peel, and slice the beets thinly.

In a bowl large enough for the sliced beets, mix the remaining ingredients thoroughly. Add the beets and let the salad marinate at least 4 hours. May be eaten at room temperature or cold.

Garlic Festival for Eight
≈ ROSINA WILSON ≈

Cajun Clams

Bagna Cauda Deluxe

Rack of Lamb Dijon

Garlic Festival Spuds

ROSINA IS unquestionably a serious garlic practitioner. A winner of the Gilroy Garlic Festival recipe contest several years back and an early member of Berkeley's Garlic Festival Committee, Rosina is loyal and articulate, and has gone on to become an important food writer in the Bay Area. Here is what Rosina says about her menu: "There's nothing like garlic for unifying a menu, and it even tops Trivial Pursuit for bringing a roomful of people together. This menu works equally well indoors or out-of-doors, as a stand-up buffet or an informal sit-down affair, depending on your mood, your furniture, and your guests. Just set out several scrap bowls for shells, bones, veggie ends, garlic skins, and such; then turn everyone loose. Enjoy!"

Cajun Clams

This recipe mutated in several stages from my entry in the 1984 Gilroy Garlic Festival cook-off finals. That one was so incendiary that it brought tears to the eyes and seared the palates of several judges, all because of a brand-new box of cayenne which packed ten times more firepower than the year-old batch I had used at home for testing. I call this new version "Cajun Clams," in deference to the flamethrowing effects of both the infamous cayenne and the Tabasco sauce.

4 cans chopped clams, drained, about 1½ cups; or the equivalent in fresh clams, steamed and chopped
20 to 30 cloves garlic, pressed, plus several cloves for garnish
½ cup butter, softened
¼ cup minced bacon
1 tablespoon fresh oregano, or 1 teaspoon dried
⅓ cup grated Parmesan cheese
¼ cup dry sherry
½ cup French bread crumbs

¾ cup chopped parsley
2 tablespoons lemon juice, plus wedges for garnish
½ cup toasted pecans, roughly chopped, plus extra whole pecans for garnish
¼ teaspoon freshly ground black pepper
¼ teaspoon cayenne, or more to taste
4 dashes Tabasco sauce, or more to taste
1 tablespoon olive oil for garnish

Mix all the ingredients except garnishes in a large bowl. Spoon the mixture generously into clam shells (saved from a previous fresh clam dinner) or purchased scallop shells. As garnish, stud each stuffed shell with a slice of garlic dipped in olive oil, a quartered pecan, and a dusting of cayenne. Bake in an oven preheated to 375° for 25 to 30 minutes, until bread crumbs turn golden brown and the center cooks through. Serve piping hot with lemon wedges.

Variation: the recipe testers tried this mixture stuffed into individual little pie shells, and it worked great!

Bagna Cauda Deluxe

Bagna cauda is Piedmontese dialect for *hot bath*. Like fondue, this Northern Italian specialty draws everyone to the communal cooking pot. The ground rules are simple: just dip a piece of vegetable or seafood into the bubbling bath, hold a slice of baguette under it to sop up any stray drops, and enjoy. After every few morsels, spear a garlic clove, smear it on the sauce-drenched bread, and start again.

Sauce:
16 tablespoons unsalted butter (2 sticks)
¾ cup olive oil
1 to 2 cups small garlic cloves, peeled

1 2-ounce can anchovies, drained and chopped, or to taste

For dipping:

1 bunch baby carrots, with leaves if possible

1 red bell pepper, sliced

1 yellow bell pepper, sliced

1 basket cherry tomatoes

1 basket yellow cherry tomatoes, if available

½ pound small, perfect button mushrooms

½ small head red cabbage, sliced down to the stem and fanned out

½ pound snow peas or edible-pod sugar snap peas

4 to 6 young, tender zucchini, in strips

2 to 3 yellow summer squash or yellow zucchini, in strips

1 bunch small radishes, with leaves

½ pound *haricots verts*, or small, firm string beans

2 bunches young, slender green onions

2 pounds shrimp, cooked and peeled

2 to 3 sweet French baguettes, thinly sliced

Early in the day, melt butter and oil together in a fondue pot or heavy saucepan. Stir in garlic cloves and simmer over lowest possible heat for several hours, until cloves become very soft and tender. Add anchovies and keep warm.

Be spontaneous with the vegetables, adapting to season and budget. Try to preserve the natural look of the vegetables by not slicing them all the way through, and arrange them cornucopia-style in a large basket or rustic serving dish.

At serving time, raise heat under sauce until mixture bubbles slightly. Gather 'round the pot and dig—or should I say dip—in!

Rack of Lamb Dijon

3 to 4 racks of lamb, 8 chops each

4 ounces (½ jar) Dijon mustard

20 to 40 large cloves garlic, pressed

½ tablespoon fresh rosemary, chopped, or 1 tablespoon dried

3 tablespoons robust red wine

1 tablespoon olive oil

½ teaspoon freshly ground black pepper

Trim lamb racks well, removing all fat. At least 4 hours before dinner, mix remaining ingredients together, and spread evenly on meat (top and sides of rack). Refrigerate lamb or keep at cool room temperature to marinate. To cook, place lamb racks in a preheated 475° oven for 15 minutes; then reduce heat to 400° for 10 minutes for medium-rare. Watch carefully to make sure the coating doesn't burn. Slice into single or double chops. Serve immediately.

Garlic Festival Spuds

In this dish, the garlic and potatoes stew together in the rich, buttery stock, and by the time the potatoes are done, the garlic is cooked through to creamy smoothness inside its skins. You can squeeze it out onto forkfuls of potato or lamb, onto bread, or straight into your mouth.

2 pounds tiny red or white "creamer" potatoes, as small as possible
12 or more small heads garlic, roots and outer skins removed, or 1½ cups small garlic cloves, peeled

4 tablespoons butter
½ cup beef or lamb stock
1 branch fresh rosemary, or 1 tablespoon dried
Salt and black pepper to taste

Scrub the potatoes; arrange in 1 layer with the garlic in a large pan or flameproof casserole. Top with chunks of butter, pour stock over, and tuck in rosemary. Cover tightly and bake in a 350° oven or cook over medium heat on top of the stove until potatoes are tender. (If anything threatens to stick, add more stock.) All the liquid should be absorbed, with a buttery glaze coating the potatoes and garlic. Adjust seasonings to taste.

Thai Menu
≈ BRUCE COST ≈

Shrimp and Fresh Water Chestnuts in Garlic-Coconut Sauce

Hot Cucumber Pickles with Garlic and Dried Shrimp

Noodles with Garlic Curry Paste, Pork, and Peanuts

BRUCE IS a marvelous cook and teacher, specializing in Asian foods. His book, Ginger East to West *(Aris Books), is a fascinating collection of information and recipes focusing on the enigmatic ginger root, which is used so often in Asian cooking in conjunction with garlic. Bruce has a particular fondness for Thai cooking, and he notes that the Thais are second in the world (after the Koreans) in per capita garlic consumption.*

Note: *The Asian ingredients called for in these recipes are readily available at Asian markets or in the Oriental foods sections of supermarkets.*

Shrimp and Fresh Water Chestnuts in Garlic-Coconut Sauce

1½ pounds medium or large
  shrimp
½ teaspoon salt
2 teaspoons cornstarch
1 teaspoon sesame oil
8 fresh water chestnuts
1¾ cup peanut oil
¾ cup minced garlic
¼ cup minced fresh red chili
  peppers, with seeds
1 stalk lemon grass, white part
  only, minced

1 14-ounce can coconut milk
14 ounces water
2 tablespoons fish sauce
2 cups chopped fresh coriander,
  leaves and stems
¼ cup freshly ground black pepper
  for garnish
1 lime, cut in wedges (alternate
  garnish)

Peel and devein the shrimp. Cut them in half lengthwise, blend with ½ teaspoon salt, the cornstarch, and sesame oil and refrigerate for at least 30 minutes. Wash the mud off the water chestnuts, peel them, cut in half, and set aside.

Heat ¼ cup of peanut oil in a wok or skillet. Add the garlic, chili peppers, and lemon grass, and stir until fragrant. Add the coconut milk and water and bring to a boil. Turn the heat to medium, add the fish sauce, and cook, stirring from time to time, until the sauce is reduced by half. It should be slightly thick and creamy. Turn off the heat and cover to keep warm.

Heat a clean wok and add 1½ cups peanut oil. When hot, add the shrimp, stirring to separate. When separated and white (no more than 30 seconds), remove shrimp with a slotted spoon and place in a colander to drain. Add the water chestnuts to the oil. Fry for 15 seconds, remove, and drain with the shrimp.

Reheat the sauce and add the shrimp and water chestnuts. Cook, stirring briefly, just until hot. Turn off the heat, stir in the coriander. Remove to a platter and serve with the pepper or lime wedges on the side.

Hot Cucumber Pickles with Garlic and Dried Shrimp

6 cucumbers
2 tablespoons coarse salt
½ cup sugar
½ cup red wine vinegar
1 tablespoon fish sauce
¼ cup peanut oil

10 small dried hot peppers
12 garlic cloves, peeled and
    smashed
4 small fresh red chili peppers, cut
    into rounds
½ cup dried shrimp, ground

Peel the cucumbers, cut them in half lengthwise, and scrape out the seeds. Slice the cucumbers thinly into "half-moons," and put them into a mixing bowl. Toss with the salt and let sit for at least an hour.

Meanwhile, mix the sugar, vinegar, and fish sauce, and set aside.

Heat the oil in a saucepan and add the dried chili peppers. When they smoke and blacken, add the garlic and the fresh chilis and cook, stirring very briefly. Add the sugar/vinegar mixture and bring to a boil. When the sugar is dissolved turn off the heat.

Squeeze the moisture from the cucumbers by wrapping them in a towel and twisting it. (You needn't leave them bone dry.) Put the cucumbers in another bowl and, when the sauce is cool, pour it over the cucumbers. Toss with the ground dried shrimp and let sit 30 minutes before serving, or refrigerate and serve as needed. These pickles will keep at least a couple of weeks.

Noodles with Garlic Curry Paste, Pork, and Peanuts

¾ cup peanut oil
¾ cup raw shelled peanuts
½ cup sliced garlic
¾-pound pork loin
2 tablespoons dark soy sauce
2 teaspoons sesame oil
½ pound fresh egg noodles (mein)
2 bunches thin scallions, cut,
    greens and all, into 1-inch
    lengths

½ cup All-Purpose Garlic Curry
    Paste (see following recipe)
½ cup chicken stock
1 to 2 teaspoons salt or to taste
    (the noodles will absorb a lot of
    salt)

Heat the peanut oil in a saucepan until nearly smoking. Add the peanuts and turn off the heat. Allow them to brown about 5 minutes in the oil as it cools. Remove with a slotted spoon to a paper towel to drain. Chop the peanuts coarsely and set aside. Reheat oil and fry garlic slices until crisp and golden, about 30 seconds. Remove with a slotted spoon and drain on a paper towel. Pour off all but 3 tablespoons of the peanut oil (save the rest for another use).

Thinly slice the pork into ovals. Stack the slices and julienne. Toss the pork with the dark soy sauce and sesame oil and set aside.

Bring a large quantity of salted water to boil. Add the noodles and cook 3½ to 4 minutes. Drain and rinse under cold water to stop the cooking. Toss with a little peanut oil and set aside.

Heat the reserved 3 tablespoons of peanut oil in a wok or large skillet. When hot, add the pork and stir until all the pieces separate and begin to color, 1 to 2 minutes. Remove to a small bowl with a slotted spoon. Add the curry paste to the oil and heat. Stir briefly and add the scallion pieces. Stir for 20 seconds and add the noodles, chicken stock, and salt. Cook stirring over high heat for 2 minutes. Add the pork and any accumulated juices and cook, stirring, just to heat thoroughly. Turn off the heat, stir in the peanuts and garlic slices, and transfer to a serving platter.

All-Purpose Garlic Curry Paste

This fiery curry paste can be used in fried rice, noodle dishes or added to soups and stews. It will keep for a couple of weeks in a jar in the refrigerator.

1 tablespoon cumin seeds
1½ tablespoons coriander seeds
1 tablespoon black peppercorns
20 cloves garlic
4 ½-inch-thick slices of ginger
15 green jalapeño chilies (or 30 small green Thai chilies)
1 bunch fresh coriander including roots (cilantro)

1 fat stalk lemon grass, bottom third
1 tablespoon fine shrimp paste (sauce)
½ cup peanut oil
¼ cup lime juice
½ teaspoon sugar
1½ teaspoons salt

Toast the cumin seeds, coriander seeds, and peppercorns in a small skillet, shaking them, until fragrant. Grind them in a spice grinder or mortar, and set aside.

Add the garlic, ginger, and chilies to the container of a food processor or mortar. Cut the coriander and lemon grass into 1-inch lengths and add them. Process to a coarse paste. Add the shrimp paste, half the oil, the lime juice, sugar, and salt, and continue to blend to a paste. Remove to a bowl and stir in the spices and the rest of the oil. After using, store the remainder in a sealed jar in the refrigerator.

South American Menu

≈ BARBARA KAROFF ≈

Spicy Empanadas

Potatoes with Garlic and Chilies

Kale with Garlic and Garlic Sausage

Garlic Flan with Sweet-Sour Orange Chili Sauce

BARBARA IS *a food writer and teacher with a fascination for the little known foods of South America. Her forthcoming book,* The Tastes of South America *(Aris Books), focuses on all the wonderful ingredients that make up these cuisines, but certainly garlic is one of the most important. Barbara says of this menu: "Although this may at first appear to be a rather unusual menu, the essentials are all included. There's meat, potatoes, and a leafy green vegetable—plus an elegant dessert. And there's garlic from start to finish."*

Spicy Empanadas

Crust:

3 ounces cream cheese cheese
½ cup butter
Dash of Tabasco sauce

2 tablespoons toasted sesame seeds
¼ cup Parmesan cheese
1 cup flour

Combine the cream cheese, butter, Tabasco sauce, sesame seeds, and Parmesan cheese by hand or in a food processor. Add the flour and combine thoroughly. Chill for 30 minutes before rolling as thinly as possible and cutting into 3-inch rounds.

Filling:

⅓ pound ground beef
1 tablespoon olive oil
½ cup finely chopped onion
12 cloves garlic, 6 minced and 6
    coarsely chopped
3 serrano or jalapeño chilies,
    seeded, finely chopped
1 tablespoon cumin seeds, crushed

Salt and pepper to taste
2 tablespoons chopped parsley
3 tablespoons chopped cilantro
2 tomatoes, peeled, seeded, finely
    chopped
½ cup raisins
24 pimento-stuffed olives

Sauté the meat in the oil until it is no longer pink. Break up the large pieces. Add the onion, garlic, chilies, cumin, salt, and pepper, and continue cooking until the onion is soft. Add the parsley, cilantro, tomatoes, and raisins and cook over medium heat until the mixture is quite dry. Cool.

Place 1 teaspoonful of the mixture on each round of dough. Top with an olive and fold the dough over. Seal the edges well with the tines of a fork. Bake the *empanadas* on a lightly oiled baking sheet at 450° for 8 to 10 minutes. Serve warm.

Makes approximately 24 *empanadas*.

Potatoes with Garlic and Chilies

This wonderfully flavorful dish comes from Peru, native habitat of the potato. Make it as hot (with chilies) or as garlicky as you like. The naturally bland potatoes can take a lot. The hot potatoes and the sauce should be combined just before serving.

3 pounds red or white new potatoes
4 to 6 cloves garlic, minced
1 onion, finely chopped
2 to 3 serrano or jalapeño chilies, seeded, finely chopped
1⅓ cups safflower oil

1 cup evaporated milk or half and half
¼ pound queso fresco or feta cheese, cubed or crumbled
3 hard-cooked eggs, coarsely chopped
Salt and pepper to taste

Scrub the potatoes and boil them in lightly salted water until they are tender. Drain them well and cut each one into bite-sized pieces.

Sauté the garlic, onion, and chilies in the oil until the onion is golden. Gradually add the milk, stirring constantly with a wooden spoon. Add the cheese, eggs, salt, and pepper (be careful with salt if using feta cheese), and mix just enough to combine. When cheese is melted, add potatoes and stir to coat thoroughly, taking care not to mash the potatoes.

Kale with Garlic and Garlic Sausage

Brazilians love kale, a green leafy vegetable often neglected in the United States. In this recipe, inspired by one that is popular in the Brazilian state of Minas Gerais, collard greens may be substituted.

2½ pounds kale
½ pound garlic sausage, cut into ¼-inch slices

Vegetable oil, if necessary
4 cloves garlic, minced

Wash the kale and trim off the stems. Blanch the greens in boiling, salted water for 2 minutes. Transfer them to a colander, refresh with cold water, and drain well. Squeeze to remove as much water as possible. Shred thinly.

Sauté the sausage (in a small amount of oil, if necessary). When it just begins to brown lightly, add the garlic and cook over medium heat until the garlic is nicely browned. Add the shredded kale and toss gently to coat. Sauté the combined ingredients until the greens are tender, about 10 minutes. Serve at once.

Garlic Flan with Sweet-Sour Orange Chili Sauce

8 to 10 large cloves garlic, coarsely
  chopped
3 cups half and half

4 eggs
Sweet-Sour Orange Chili Sauce
  (see recipe below)

Add garlic to the half and half in a saucepan and heat the liquid slowly until it is just about to boil. Remove it from the heat and allow to cool to room temperature. Beat the eggs and add them to the cooled half and half. Strain the mixture into 6 individual baking dishes. Place them in a pan and add hot water to come halfway up the sides of the dishes. Bake at 325° for about 30 minutes or until the custard is set and a knife inserted into the center comes out clean. Remove the dishes from the water bath and cool to room temperature.

Sweet-Sour Orange Chili Sauce:

½ cup sugar
1 teaspoon cornstarch
⅓ cup boiling water
1 tablespoon minced Anaheim or
  Poblano chili peppers

2 tablespoons lemon juice
1 teaspoon finely grated orange
  peel

Combine the sugar and cornstarch in a saucepan. Add the boiling water. Return to a boil, and then simmer, stirring occasionally, until the mixture thickens slightly. Cool to room temperature and stir in the chili peppers, lemon juice, and orange peel. Divide the sauce among 6 serving plates and unmold the flans on top. Serve at room temperature.

Spring Menu

Garlic Oyster Soufflé

Napa Valley Butterflied Leg of Lamb

Spinach and Radicchio Salad with Garlic Vinaigrette

Figs in Wine and Honey

THIS SPRING *menu would be appropriate for a special Easter meal. As lovers of the stinking rose, we always look for opportunities to enliven holidays with the addition of garlic to the repetitive dishes of our childhood. These foods really are transformed by adding garlic. When you think about it, it seems obvious that traditional*

American holiday meals would reflect the anti-garlic prejudice inherited from our forefathers. Adding garlicky dishes to our holiday meals is a way of recreating our traditions to suit our true American melting-pot tastes.

Garlic Oyster Soufflé
≈ NATASHA GRANOFF ≈

Natasha, Aris' recipe tester, created this delicious mix of oysters, garlic, and cheese, all in a rich soufflé.

1½ cups milk
Bouquet garni: 2 sprigs thyme, 2
  sprigs parsley, 1 bay leaf,
  3 peppercorns
1 cup garlic cloves, peeled
4 tablespoons butter
¼ pound Parmesan cheese, grated
3 tablespoons flour

4 egg yolks
6 large, fresh oysters (or one 10-
  ounce bottle oysters), quartered
½ teaspoon salt
6 egg whites
½ pound Gruyère (or other Swiss)
  cheese, grated

Scald milk with bouquet garni. Steep 15 minutes; strain. Set aside. Cook ½ cup of the whole garlic cloves in the butter until soft and golden. Drain cloves and reserve butter. Puree cooked garlic with the remaining raw garlic. Set aside.

Butter a two quart soufflé dish. Sprinkle bottom and sides with half the Parmesan cheese.

Preheat oven to 400°.

Whisk flour into remaining butter and cook the resulting *roux* for 2 minutes. Whisk the scalded milk into the *roux*. Cook over low heat, stirring constantly until thick. Remove from heat and whisk in egg yolks, puréed garlic, and oysters. Beat egg whites to soft peaks. Fold a quarter of the whites into the mixture, add Gruyère, and carefully fold in remaining whites. Pour into buttered dish and sprinkle with remaining Parmesan. Bake in 400° oven for 25 to 35 minutes, or until set and golden.

Napa Valley Butterflied Leg of Lamb
≈ NARSAI'S RESTAURANT ≈

A fixture in the Bay Area for many years, Narsai's was a pioneering restaurant that raised culinary consciousness immeasurably. Now that the restaurant is closed, Narsai David continues his culinary journey through catering, cookbooks, and other ventures. His support of The Berkeley Garlic Festival continues to be much appreciated.

5- to 6-pound leg of lamb,
   butterflied

Marinade:

2 medium onions, roughly
   chopped
10 or more large cloves garlic,
   peeled
1 teaspoon salt
½ teaspoon black pepper
½ cup medium or dry sherry

¼ cup brandy
1 teaspoon ground cumin
1 teaspoon dried rosemary or 2
   sprigs fresh rosemary, 3 inches
   long
2 to 3 sprigs fresh marigold leaves
   (optional)

Purée marinade ingredients in a food processor or blender. Place the leg of lamb in a 10-by-14-inch roasting pan and pour the marinade over the lamb, turning to coat all surfaces. Marinate for 8 to 10 hours at room temperature or in the refrigerator for 1 to 2 days.

Broil or grill the meat, turning frequently to brown evenly. The meat is best when cooked medium-rare and will take approximately 15 to 30 minutes, depending on the heat source and the thickness of the lamb. Slice thickly and serve. The remaining marinade can be heated and combined with lamb juices after the meat is sliced, and served as a sauce.

Spinach and Radicchio Salad with Garlic Vinaigrette

1 bunch spinach
1 head radicchio
Garlic Vinaigrette (recipe follows)

Wash spinach carefully. Trim stems, keeping the leaves whole.

Separate the radicchio head into leaves. Toss together the spinach and radicchio with the Garlic Vinaigrette.

Garlic Vinaigrette:

½ cup olive oil
3 tablespoons red wine vinegar
½ teaspoon salt

⅛ teaspoon pepper
2 or more cloves garlic

Whip all ingredients in blender until smooth.

Figs in Wine and Honey

One of our recipe testers, Irene Chriss, adapted this recipe from a dessert at Chez Panisse.

1 pound dried California Mission
   figs
1 bottle red Zinfandel wine
¾ cup honey

2 sprigs fresh thyme
5 large cloves garlic, peeled
Crème fraîche or heavy cream

Combine all ingredients in a large saucepan except crème fraîche. Bring to a simmer and cook until figs are tender, about 1 hour. Remove figs; purée cooking liquid and garlic in a food processor. Return the liquid to the saucepan and reduce by half. Top figs with reduced sauce.

Serve cold, at room temperature, or warm with crème fraîche or heavy cream. Another presentation: Reduce sauce, pour some onto a dessert plate, top with figs, and surround with the cream.

Thanksgiving Menu

Roasted Pumpkin and Garlic Soup with Pepper Croutons

Stuffed Game Hens

Snow Peas with Garlic and Lemon

Baked Yams with Garlic, Honey, and Apricots

THE SACRED Thanksgiving dinner. Woe to those who would tinker with this most cherished of all American meals. Yet the fact is that there is no single Thanksgiving meal, but countless millions of meals based on the histories of each family in America. One food historian can tell you exactly where you grew up if you tell him what you ate for Thanksgiving as a child. He found that people "must" have things exactly as they did as children or else it doesn't taste "good." Our contention is that once you have tried our garlic Thanksgiving menu, you will find the will power to depart from, at least occassionally, your Thanksgiving ritual. We will not ask you to give up the standard pumpkin or mincemeat pie, although you could add a garlic undercurrent to the whipped cream served with the pie. And if you are really motivated, you can add garlic to your homemade mincemeat.

Roasted Pumpkin Garlic Soup with Pepper Croutons
≈ JUDY ROGERS ≈

Judy is one of the finest young cooks in the Bay Area. She was previously a chef at Chez Panisse and at the Union Hotel in Benicia, California. Pumpkin's affinity for garlic is made deliciously clear by this recipe.

1 small, firm pumpkin (about 6 pounds) or yellow squash split in half, fibers and seeds removed
2 tablespoons unsalted butter, softened
Salt
1 to 4 heads small-cloved red garlic, separated, unpeeled
4 sprigs thyme
1 to 3 cups rich poultry stock
4 to 6 tablespoons unsalted butter
Fresh thyme, chopped for garnish
Pepper Croutons (see following recipe)

Preheat oven to 350°.

Rub pumpkin cavities liberally with 2 tablespoons of softened butter, and then salt. Put garlic cloves on a heavy baking sheet in 2 piles and bury 2 sprigs of thyme in each one. Place a pumpkin half over each pile of garlic and put in preheated oven. Roast until the pumpkin skin begins to blister and flesh softens, about 1½ hours. Remove from the oven and cool until the pumpkin can be handled easily.

Peel the skin from pumpkin and discard. Press the pulp through a food mill or purée in a food processor, being careful not to overprocess. Gather garlic cloves and any juices from the pumpkin and press through the food mill or through a sieve with a bit of warm stock. Stir garlic and pumpkin together in a heavy soup pot over low heat. Add enough warm stock to achieve desired consistency. Season with salt to taste. To serve, stir in 4 to 6 tablespoons butter and garnish with chopped thyme and croutons.

Pepper Croutons:
2 slices firm white bread, cut into ½-inch cubes
¼ teaspoon freshly ground black pepper
Salt to taste
1½ tablespoons unsalted butter

Let bread cubes dry out at room temperature for about 15 minutes. Sprinkle the bread cubes with the pepper and salt. In a small frying pan, melt the butter and add the bread cubes, tossing constantly over medium-high heat until croutons are crisp and golden, about 3 minutes.

Stuffed Game Hens
≈ IRENE CHRISS ≈

While testing recipes for this book, Irene couldn't resist offering us some of her own garlicky creations. Here is one that we couldn't resist offering you.

2 Cornish game hens
1 pound boned, cubed chicken
   thigh with skin
½ pound ground seasoned sausage
   (a good quality sausage found in
   specialty markets is best; sausages with garlic, basil, fennel, or
   other herbs enhance this recipe)
6 ounces ground veal
1 egg
1 tablespoon *quatre épices* (a mixture
   of white pepper, black pepper,
   coriander seeds, ginger, and
   cloves)

¼ cup shelled pistachio nuts
¼ to ½ cup cognac
20 cloves garlic, minced
1 tablespoon chopped parsley
1 slice quality ham, ¼-inch thick
   (optional)
Olive oil
Salt and pepper to taste

Have your butcher bone the Cornish game hens, leaving the skin, wings, and leg bones in place. Lay the boned hens out flat, skin-side down.

In a food processor, finely grind the chicken thighs and skin. Add the sausage, veal, and egg and combine very well. Remove the mixture to a bowl and add spices, pistachio nuts, cognac, garlic, parsley, and optional ham. Season with salt and pepper. (Optional: To enhance the flavor of this stuffing, marinate by sprinkling with some additional cognac. Refrigerate for 6 to 24 hours.)

Divide the stuffing mixture in half and spread on each game hen, taking care to tuck the mixture into the boned thigh cavity. Be sure the mixture is spread evenly on the surface of each bird. Lift both sides of the skin to overlap and close the hens. Turn the hens over (breast-side up) and reshape them to resemble their original form. Turn the hens over again and sew with needle and thread or with trussing needle and kitchen twine. Turn each hen on its back again and the tuck wings under bird; tie up the legs. Lightly coat with olive oil and add salt and pepper.

Place the hens on a roasting pan and bake in a preheated 400° oven for 10 minutes; then turn heat down to 350° for approximately 1 hour, or until the skin is nicely browned and slightly crisp, and the juices run clear. Baste the hens occasionally while baking.

To serve hot: Remove trussing, cut each hen in half lengthwise, and place on a dinner plate.

To serve cold: Cool the hens, remove trussing, cover, and chill. Cut the birds in half lengthwise just before serving.

Snow Peas with Garlic and Lemon
≈ NATASHA GRANOFF ≈

This is a simple but surprisingly interesting dish. The garlic should be sliced paper-thin along the length of the cloves. The slices become translucent and limp, clinging to the snow peas.

1 pound snow peas
2 tablespoons olive oil
2 tablespoons butter
10 cloves garlic, peeled, thinly
    sliced lengthwise

Grated rind of a lemon
Juice of ½ lemon
Salt and pepper to taste

Wash and string the peas. Blanch in boiling water for 45 seconds until bright green but still crisp. Refresh under cold water, drain. Heat olive oil and butter over low heat and sauté garlic until just turning golden. Toss in lemon rind, lemon juice, snow peas, and salt and pepper to taste. Heat through and serve.

Baked Yams with Garlic, Honey, and Apricots
≈ NATASHA GRANOFF ≈

The sweet, caramelized garlic is a wonderful touch with traditional holiday yam dishes.

4 medium yams
½ cup garlic cloves, finely chopped
4 tablespoons butter (½ stick)

⅓ cup honey
½ cup dried apricots, julienned
Rind and juice of one orange

Boil yams until tender, about 30 minutes. Drain, peel, and cut in half lengthwise and again crosswise in ¼-inch slices. Fan out in a buttered gratin or casserole dish. Sprinkle garlic over yams. In a small saucepan melt the butter with the honey, apricots, and orange rind. Cook for 1 or 2 minutes and pour over the yams. Add orange juice to bottom of dish, without it touching the yams. Bake in a preheated 350° oven for 30 to 35 minutes.

Christmas Menu

Garlic-Stuffed Prunes

Wild Mushroom and Garlic Soup

Roast Pork with Garlic Applesauce

Garlic Cheese Biscuits

Garlic Frosted Grapes

Garlic-Stuffed Prunes
≈ IRENE CHRISS ≈

This garlicky hors d'oeuvre may be prepared in advance and heated at the last moment as guests arrive. It is a perfect accompaniment for cocktails and an excellent dish to serve for a buffet.

30 small cloves garlic, unpeeled
8 tablespoons butter (1 stick)
8 ounces cream cheese (without gum)
2 tablespoons garlic purée (see page 40)

30 pitted prunes, plumped by steeping in tea, wine, or warm water
8 strips of bacon

Blanch whole cloves of garlic in boiling water for 5 to 10 minutes. Rinse garlic in cool water and "pop out" the cloves. Roast cloves in butter in a 400° oven until golden, about 30 to 40 minutes. Combine cream cheese and garlic purée. Make an incision in plumped prunes and stuff with cheese mixture and a roasted garlic clove. Squeeze the prunes closed. Cut bacon strips in half width-wise and then lengthwise, and then wrap one strip around each prune.

Broil prunes until bacon is crisp, about 4 minutes. Insert a toothpick and pass the hors d'oeuvres warm.

Wild Mushroom and Garlic Soup
≈ POULET ≈

Poulet is one of Berkeley's liveliest fine-food delis. Each year during The Berkeley Garlic Festival, Poulet has its own mini-festival. Here's a wonderfully rich recipe from their first festival dinner, created by Bruce Aidells and first published in Garlic Times. *It can be served with or without a puff-pastry top. (A special thanks to Shai Yerlick, Poulet's chef, and to Poulet's owner, Marilyn Rinzler, for their continued support in making Berkeley the garlic-eating capital of America!)*

2 cups water
¼ cup dry sherry
6 to 8 dried wild mushrooms
  (cèpes or morels)
1 large onion, sliced
1 cup coarsely chopped garlic (15
  to 20 cloves)
4 tablespoons butter (½ stick)

6 cups rich chicken stock
½ cup dry white wine

Garnish:
½ cup sour cream (or crème
  fraîche)
2 tablespoons minced garlic
1 tablespoon minced parsley

Boil water and sherry, and pour over mushrooms; soak for several hours. In a soup pot, sauté onions and garlic in the butter until they are golden. Add stock and wine. Simmer for 30 minutes. Purée onions and garlic in 1 cup of the broth and return to the pot. Drain mushrooms, chop finely, and add them with their soaking liquid to the pot. Simmer for 15 minutes.

To serve, ladle soup into bowls garnished with a dollop of sour cream mixed with minced garlic. Sprinkle parsley over the top.

Variation with puff pastry:
½ cup sour cream (or crème
  fraîche)
2 tablespoons cornstarch
2 tablespoons minced garlic

1 pound puff pastry
2 egg yolks whisked with 1
  tablespoon water

Allow soup to cool thoroughly. Combine sour cream and cornstarch, and whisk into soup. Ladle soup into 6 individual oven-proof bowls. Divide the minced garlic among the bowls. Roll out the puff pastry ¼-inch thick. Cut 6 circles whose diameters are 2 inches longer than those of the soup bowls. Place a circle over each bowl and brush with egg yolk. Refrigerate 30 minutes. Place bowls well apart on a sheet pan. Bake in a 400° oven for 15 to 20 minutes until pastry is puffed and golden.

Roast Pork with Garlic Applesauce

Garlic and apples are a wonderful combination. Here, the roasted garlic from the pork is combined with homemade applesauce to create a spicy apple side dish.

2- to 3-pound pork loin, boned,
   stuffed with peeled garlic
   cloves, and tied up
3 sprigs fresh rosemary (or
   1 tablespoon dried)
½ cup minced parsley
10 to 15 cloves garlic, pressed

1 cup very fine bread crumbs
½ teaspoon salt
¼ teaspoon pepper
½ to ¾ cup olive oil
20 cloves garlic (2 heads), root-
   end cut off, broken apart
Applesauce (see following recipe)

One day in advance, prepare the pork, then combine finely chopped fresh rosemary (if using dried rosemary, crumble between your palms), parsley, pressed garlic, bread crumbs, salt, and pepper. Whisk in enough olive oil to make a spreadable paste. Score fat on loin, and mask pork loin with herb paste. Set pork loin on a rack in a roasting pan; cover and refrigerate overnight. Let meat come to room temperature (approximately 2 to 3 hours) before roasting.

Preheat oven to 400°. Add water to cover bottom of roasting pan. Roast pork loin at 400° for 30 minutes. Reduce heat to 375°. Add 20 cloves of garlic to pan and finish cooking, approximately 1 hour, or until a meat thermometer inserted in the middle of the pork loin registers 170°. While pork is cooking, make Applesauce.

Applesauce:

¼ stick butter
2 pounds pippin apples, pared,
   cored, and cut into bite size
   pieces

¼ cup water or apple cider
2 tablespoons sugar (optional)
Garlic cloves from roasting pan

Melt butter in a large pot. Add apples and water. Cover and cook over low heat until apples are soft, about 30 minutes. Add sugar. When pork is done, remove the garlic from bottom of pan, "pop out" the cloves, and mix into the applesauce. Serve on the side.

Garlic Cheese Biscuits
≈ IRENE CHRISS ≈

These biscuits have a wonderful aftertaste—very mild. They're great with soup, salad, or with wine for hors d'oeuvres.

1 cup all-purpose flour
½ teaspoon salt
½ teaspoon paprika
Freshly ground pepper to taste
½ cup unsalted butter, softened
3 tablespoons garlic purée (3 large cloves)
⅓ cup grated Parmesan cheese

4 ounces very sharp cheddar, grated
3 tablespoons Garlic Chips (see following recipe)
2 tablespoons heavy cream, chilled
1 egg

In a food processor (or by hand), blend the flour, salt, paprika, and pepper. Mix the butter and 2 tablespoons of the garlic purée, and then cut garlic butter into flour mixture until it resembles coarse meal. Add the cheeses, garlic chips, and cream and mix until a smooth dough is formed. Chill for at least 1 hour.

Roll the dough so it is between ¼- and ½-inch thick. Cut into rectangles that are approximately ½ inch by 3 inches. Paint the rectangles with the egg, beaten with 1 tablespoon garlic purée, and then place them on ungreased cookie sheets.

Place the cookie sheets in a 350° oven and bake for 15 to 20 minutes, depending on the thickness of the biscuits, or until the biscuits turn a golden brown and puff slightly. Eat the biscuits while they are warm or serve them at room temperature.

Makes approximately 24 biscuits.

Garlic Chips:
3 large cloves garlic
1 tablespoon butter

Slice cloves of garlic into slivers. Sauté over medium-high heat until slivers are crisp and brown.

Garlic Frosted Grapes

If you can't bring yourself to eat these, you can hang them on your Christmas tree. Actually, they are quite good, and you can also use this recipe with strawberries and cherries.

6 cloves garlic
2 cups granulated sugar
1 egg white

1 pound red seedless grapes, the bigger the better

One day ahead, sliver garlic cloves and toss with sugar. Store in an air-tight container. On the next day, sieve out the garlic. Wash the grapes and pat them dry. Lightly beat the egg white and, with a pastry brush, paint the grapes thoroughly. Toss the grapes in the garlic sugar and let dry on a sheet pan for 1 hour. Place in refrigerator or freezer until the grapes are chilled. Serve frosty.

A Spanish Gypsy in a Berkeley Kitchen

≈ PAT DARROW ≈

NO ONE *I have met in the last 15 years has displayed a greater affinity for and appreciation of garlic than Anzonini del Puerto, a Gypsy from southern Spain. Anzonini lived in Berkeley for several years beginning in the late 1970s, and his native attraction to garlic was an inspiration to dozens of cooks and to hundreds of admirers of his flamenco concerts—which were inevitably given in the context of fiestas, complete with vast quantities of food prepared, usually, by Anzonini.*

I remember meeting Anzonini at his first concert in Berkeley. (Anzonini had many fans in Berkeley who had met him in Spain. He came to Berkeley to visit his friends and give concerts.) He laughed when he learned I had written a book on garlic because he couldn't conceive of food without garlic, so why all the fuss? Nonetheless, garlic was the theme of his cooking in Berkeley, or so he led me to believe. My friend, Pat Darrow, was so enthralled by Anzonini's concert and food that she honored him by handing over the sterling-silver garlic amulet I once gave her. From that day on, Anzonini never removed the garlic charm from his charm necklace, and his bond with Pat was sealed. They lived as man and wife for five years.

While visiting Spain in 1983, Anzonini had a stroke and died. Although he had been in failing health for some time, Anzonini's death was a big shock. Before he had left for Spain, he and Pat had been working on a book of his recipes, but with his passing, the book project was set aside. Nevertheless, Pat has written a short essay on Anzonini's cooking, and I think it paints an interesting portrait of what is essentially a peasant cuisine—hearty, simple, yet artful. And in no small way, it keeps the marvelous memories alive.

(If you would like a glimpse of Anzonini's music and dance, you can see him perform in Les Blank's film, Garlic Is as Good as Ten Mothers, *which is available on video cassette from LSR—see page 114.)*

F OR OVER four years, while interest in garlic was growing after the publication of *The Book of Garlic* and the production of the film *Garlic Is as Good as Ten Mothers,* a Spanish Gypsy flamenco dancer, Anzonini del Puerto, was cooking in my small Berkeley kitchen as he had cooked all his life in Spain, using quantities of garlic that astounded the most avid lovers of the stinking rose.

Anzonini wanted everyone he met to taste his food, and he invited old friends, new friends, dance students, and clients of his small sausage business (including many of the finest professional and amateur cooks in the Bay Area) to eat with us and watch him cook.

Anzonini's dance gestures and witty Spanish songs, for which he was well known in Spain, brought an air of art and performance to the kitchen that had become his stage. Hanging braids of garlic, chorizo, branches of bay, and old Spanish posters and photos transformed the kitchen into a set for Anzonini's unique drama. It was a nervous drama, its apparent spontaneity masking an absolute commitment to peasant food made with the fresh ingredients native to Andalucia and the cooking methods of his Gypsy family.

For those of us watching, Anzonini's charisma, his rhythmic Spanish in a rasping rat-a-tat voice, and the unfamiliar flavors and smells made the scene exciting and somehow precarious. In retrospect, I realize that he worked, from long experience, with deliberateness and sureness: never spilling, never cutting himself, never hesitating, and especially never hurrying. He combined ingredients that were familiar to us and, using unfamiliar methods, transformed them into new and unusual dishes that were complex, finished, and deeply satisfying.

Anzonini used the ingredients of Andalucia: garbanzo beans, lentils, bacalao (dried salt cod), fresh seafood, meat or chicken, eggs, vegetables, rice, and potatoes, always cooked with enormous amounts of garlic and olive oil, and often also with onions, tomatoes, and green peppers. His seasonings were bay leaves, cloves, and black pepper, and in a few recipes, oregano, nutmeg, or parsley. In some of his most distinctive dishes, like Potage Andaluz (a meat-laden garbanzo soup), he added *pimentos molidos* (a mild ground chili powder similar to paprika). Salt was always important, especially in the peasant soups which used water rather than stock.

He prepared his ingredients differently than we do. Garlic was sliced very thin, almost never chopped. Tomatoes were sliced, never peeled or seeded. The vegetables for a sauce (garlic, onions, green pepper, and tomato) were not sautéed separately but added all together to the smoking-hot oil. Meat, seafood or skinned chicken was cut into smallish pieces (by our standards) and added raw to the bubbling sauce.

After cleaning and scraping off the scales of a fresh fish, he washed it in cold water, salted it, and let it sit for an hour before cooking. Potatoes were washed and salted before frying. Eggs for tortillas were beaten on a flat plate and salted before cooking. He did not measure anything. Many of these idio-syncracies must have originated through necessity—the household in which he grew up was very large (over 50 members of his family lived and ate to-gether), and poverty and food shortages must have required ingenuity to pro-duce food so memorable that Anzonini directed all his skill and art in the kitchen to duplicating that food. The result was a unique blend of flavors that had not been set by sautéing separately, but which had released their essences in combination. The sauces or soups were as rich as the meat or seafood in them and stretched infinitely to satisfy extra guests.

Almost all of Anzonini's recipes may be categorized under four headings: *las sopas* (soups), *comida en sofrito* (foods cooked in fried tomato sauce), *comida al jerez* (foods sautéed with sherry), and *frito* (fried). Some of the wonderful and distinctive dishes he prepared that do not allow such categorizing are Gazpa-cho; Cazon en Adobo (shark marinated in vinegar, garlic, and chili powder, and dredged in flour and fried in olive oil); roasted meats or fish; and a wonderful potato salad made with lots of garlic, olive oil, and mayonnaise.

Las Sopas

Most of Anzonini's soups were made by simmering the raw ingredients to-gether in water with olive oil, garlic, onion, tomato, and green pepper at high heat for a long time. The pot was usually uncovered (or half-covered to prevent splashing), and he stirred it often and added water to the original depth when it went down.

The bread soups, Sopa de Ajo and Sopa de Tomate, were quick and deft in comparison. Garlic was fried in olive oil or a *sofrito* with lots of tomato was made; bread was fried in either of these bases, water was added and cooked down quickly, and the soup was served with a raw egg mixed in.

Ajo Caliento (hot garlic), standing somewhere between Gazpacho and Sopa de Tomate and made with the same ingredients, is an unusual dish. With a pestle, enormous amounts of garlic are mashed in a large wooden bowl with olive oil, salt, and tomatoes. Dried bread and roasted peppers are added and boiling water is poured over all the ingredients. The bowl is covered for 10 minutes and then the soup is ready to serve.

Potage Andaluz de Anzonini

This recipe will serve from 25 to 30 people. It is marvelous party fare when people will be drinking a lot.

3 pounds garbanzo beans that have been soaked overnight
2 pounds tomatoes, quartered
2 green bell peppers, cut in wide strips
2 large onions, quartered
6 whole garlic heads, excess skins removed and roots scrubbed
5 bay leaves
10 whole cloves

12 to 15 whole black peppercorns
4 tablespoons chili powder
4- to 5-pound pork butt, cubed
8 quarts cold water
1½ cups olive oil
4 Spanish chorizos, sliced thick (optional)
3 *morcillas* (Spanish blood sausage), sliced thick (optional)
Salt to taste

Place the first 12 ingredients in a large pot, or divide into two smaller pots. Bring to a boil and simmer fast for about 2 hours, or until the garbanzo beans are tender. Stir often and replace the water to the original depth with boiling water when necessary.

Add the chorizos, *morcillas*, and salt and continue simmering for 10 minutes. Serve with plenty of good crusty bread.

Comida en Sofrito

The variety of foods that Anzonini cooked in a *sofrito* included fish, pork, chicken, tongue, calamari, meatballs, *bacalao*, oxtails, and vegetables. *Sofrito* is the base for Paella and Huevos Flamenca (eggs baked in a *sofrito* to which has been added ham, chorizo, and vegetables).

Calamari Relleno

This recipe serves from 6 to 12 people, depending on what other courses are served.

12 calamari, cleaned, with tentacles removed and saved

Sofrito:
⅔ cup olive oil
6 large tomatoes, sliced
1 green bell pepper, chopped
1 medium onion, chopped

8 garlic cloves, peeled and sliced
2 bay leaves
4 whole cloves
8 peppercorns

To make the *sofrito*, pour the olive oil into a Dutch oven large enough to hold the calamari. Heat until smoke begins to form. Add the vegetables immediately and cook them until they begin to soften. Add the seasonings and cook until a sauce is achieved. Add the water and simmer while preparing the stuffing for the calamari.

Stuffing:

Calamari tentacles, chopped
4 garlic cloves, minced
½ cup chopped flat-leaf parsley
½ onion, minced
1 cup bread crumbs
3 hard-cooked eggs, chopped

½ teaspoon salt
Sofrito or white wine
1 cup light sherry or dry white wine
Water (optional)
Salt to taste

Mix together all the ingredients and moisten very lightly with some of the *sofrito* or white wine. Fill the calamari and fasten the ends with a tooth pick.

In a large skillet, place the calamari in the *sofrito*. Add the sherry or dry white wine and simmer for 30 minutes or longer, until the calamari are tender. Add water if necessary and more salt to taste.

Comida al Jerez

Jerez is *sherry* in Spanish and the name of the town in the center of the area that produces this wine. To prepare the dishes with this name, meat, chicken, and seafood or vegetables are sautéed in olive oil and garlic until nearly done; sherry is added, and the whole is cooked at high heat just until the alcohol evaporates and a sauce is achieved. It is a quick and simple method of obtaining a rich, well-finished sauce.

A popular *tapa* everywhere in Spain is mushrooms or shrimp cooked in small brown earthenware dishes by this method. These *tapas* are called *ajillo* because of the large amount of garlic in them.

Higado de Pollo al Jerez

An appetizer, or *tapa*, that serves from 6 to 10 people.

1½ pounds chicken livers
⅔ cup olive oil
8 to 10 garlic cloves, peeled and sliced thin

2 bay leaves
⅔ to 1 cup dry sherry
Salt to taste

Clean the chicken livers, then cut them in half, wash, and dry very well. Heat the oil in a skillet and add the garlic and bay leaves. Sauté until the garlic just barely begins to turn gold. Add the chicken livers and sauté on high heat for 3 to 4 minutes. Add the sherry and cook at high heat 3-4 minutes or until the livers and sauce are done. Salt and serve with good bread for soaking up the sauce.

Frito

Frito, meaning *fried* in Spanish, is a simple method Anzonini used to produce his most unique and unusual dishes—Coliflori Gitano and Berenjena Frita. Eggplant and cauliflower (or even pumpkin) were boiled until they were soft and then mashed. Enormous amounts of garlic were browned in olive oil, and the vegetables were added and fried until they absorbed the garlic and oil. The plainest food that Anzonini cooked also belongs in this category, but since there was no garlic in his fried potatoes or fried fish, songs to these simple foods will not be sung here.

Berenjena Frita con Ajo

This can be served at a party as a spread with good bread.

3 medium eggplants
¾ to 1 cup olive oil
10 garlic cloves, peeled and sliced
  thin
1 bay leaf

2 eggs
Salt and pepper to taste
Juice of 1 lemon or to taste
  (optional)

Peel the eggplants and cut them into pieces. Boil the pieces in water until they are very soft. Drain well, mash, and set aside.

Heat the oil in a large skillet. Add the garlic and bay leaf and fry until the garlic is golden brown. Remove the bay leaf. Add the eggplants and fry for about 10 minutes, stirring. Beat the eggs on a flat plate, slide them into the frying mixture, and stir well. Add salt and, if you like, the juice of one lemon. Serve hot or at room temperature.

〜

Bruschetta: The Ultimate Garlic Bread

≈ S. IRENE VIRBILA ≈

EVEN BEFORE I became a lifetime member of Lovers of the Stinking Rose, I liked the taste of garlic. No need to convince me that fresh garlic is better than garlic salt or that you usually need a lot more then any recipe writer is willing to commit to print. When I made garlic bread, I made it with fresh garlic and thought it was shockingly potent, that is, until an old man in the Tuscan village of Sorano offered to make me *bruschetta*.

The unsalted bread came from the local *fornaio*, which still used a wood-fired oven. He sat us at the table, gave the embers in his fireplace a good stir, and then cut several thick slices from a loaf of bread. Foraging around in his pantry, he came back bearing a plate of his home-cured olives and a bottle of the clear dark oil from his own olive trees on the outskirts of the village. After he grilled the bread over the embers, he rubbed each slice with a peeled clove of garlic until it disappeared. Then he drenched each piece of bread with his olive oil and motioned us to eat. This *bruschetta*—made with the simplest of ingredients—was delicious eaten with his dark salty olives and the simple wine.

Like roasted chestnuts, *bruschetta* is a great dish to make during the colder months when you're likely to have a fire going. But it also makes a quick and easy first course in summer when people mill around the barbecue. In Tuscany and Lazio, it turns up all through the year as a first course or as a *merenda*, or Tuscan snack. Instead of the French schoolchild's *pain au chocolat*, Tuscan kids like *bruschetta* (sometimes dribbled with a little vinegar, too) at their mid-afternoon (and even mid-morning) break. Inspired by this first sampling, I went to the area where the very best Tuscan olive oil is produced to find out something of the tradition of *bruschetta* in Tuscany. This is the stretch of countryside between Siena and Florence also known as *chianti classico* country. There I visited the chianti estate Badia a Coltibuono and talked with Lorenza Stucchi-Prinetti, food writer and cooking teacher, who, with her husband Piero, produces one of the finest estate-bottled olive oils imported into this country.

A great fan of *bruschetta*, she told me that the word comes from *bruciare*, to scorch or burn. Then she described the best way to make it. Listen to the details:

Start with day-old country-style bread. Slice it very thick (an inch to an inch and a half) so that when the bread is grilled, it will be crusty outside, yet soft inside. This is very important in making good *bruschetta*. Traditionally the bread is grilled over the embers in the fireplace. (My note: a broiler or toaster-oven will do fine as well, but you won't get that smoky, charred taste. In summer, use the barbecue, fired with mesquite for mesquite lovers.)

When it is well-toasted on both sides, rub the toast with fresh sweet garlic, one clove for each piece of bread, until it disappears into the bread. And if you really like garlic a lot, rub both sides of the bread.

She explained that in the countryside, Tuscan bread is traditionally baked from an unsalted dough so that the bread keeps longer. She sprinkles salt over her bread, and then freshly ground black pepper. (In California, go sparingly on the salt, and use kosher salt, if possible.) Then, she takes her deep green olive oil, with the sharp pepperiness so characteristic of Tuscan oils, and pours it over the *bruschetta* with a lavish hand.

That's the classic, but variations abound. When tomatoes are in season, she might top the *bruschetta* with a slice or two of fresh ripe tomatoes—an idea borrowed from the peasants who used to rub a tomato into extra-stale bread in order to soften it. If you've got a great tomato, this can be delicious.

Yet another variation involves heaping a tasty *fagioli*, or bean, stew on top (see Bob Waks' recipe for *fettunta*, following). In a version that is very typical of Chianti, the toasted bread is topped with boiled *cavolo nero*, a long "black" cabbage, which looks more like a cousin of Swiss chard than anything else. Curly-topped Savoy cabbage is closest to it in flavor. Because in Tuscany, she says, *bruschetta* with *cavolo nero* is considered a very poor dish, it's something, however delicious, that you would never find in a *trattoria* or restaurant.

The very best time for *bruschetta*, she told me, is in January just after the new oil has been pressed. While the oil is practically still running from the stone *frantoio*, Tuscans make an entire festive meal around *bruschetta*. Lavished with pungent *olio nuovo*, it is a special treat. The idea is to keep a constant flow of toasted bread and chianti coming. Garlic cloves, cruets of new oil, and plates of *cavolo nero* and the savory bean stew are set out on the table so that guests can "condiment" their *bruschetta* however they like.

She also makes an unusual *bruschetta* topped with fresh cheese and honey, an unexpectedly good combination of flavors.

In Barcelona, I discovered yet another version called *pa amb tomaquet*. Since the menu at the restaurant was all in Catalan, not even a Spanish translation, it took some time to decipher it. While we were puzzling it out, the waiter brought out a small bowl filled with halved tomatoes and whole garlic cloves. Fast on its heels came a platter of thick grilled country bread and cruet of olive oil.

He showed us what to do: rub the garlic over the hot toast, then rub the tomato into it until the bread takes on a bright red stain. Pour olive oil over. Sound familiar?

Reading Patrick O'Brien's biography of Picasso, I found that the Spanish painter had a special affection for the Spanish version of *bruschetta*: "When he went to the mill, people there would give him their particular delicacy, a great round of dark country bread, toasted, set to swim in the virgin oil, fished out when it began to sink, rubbed with garlic, sprinkled with salt and eaten on the spot."

All over the Mediterranean, wherever olive oil is pressed, you'll find this simple, astoundingly good dish. In Provence, they used to make something called *roustido dou moulin*, which the landowner offered to the olive pickers after the oil was pressed. This was much the same as the Italian or Spanish versions, except that it was topped with crushed anchovies.

These are all strong, bracing versions of the "garlic bread" we all grew up eating in pizza parlors and Italian-American restaurants. No one's saying you have to give up that comforting childhood taste, but it is interesting to get back to the roots of the dish, so to speak, and discover what the real thing is all about.

Fettunta

Bob Waks, a member of The Cheese Board collective in Berkeley, California, came back from a 6-week bicycle trip through Italy with this variation on *bruschetta*. He encountered it in Florence, where it is called *fettunta* (as in "oiled" or "annointed" bread). Whatever you call it, it makes a hearty snack topped with sautéed bitter greens, stewed white beans, and a sharp *grana*, or grating cheese.

2 cups white navy beans
A prosciutto or ham bone
   (optional)
1 bay leaf
10 garlic cloves, minced
1 large onion, minced
1 16-ounce can whole tomatoes,
   drained and chopped, reserving
   juice
Salt and freshly ground pepper to
   taste
1 tablespoon chopped fresh
   oregano
¼ cup chopped flat-leaved parsley

1 bunch greens (kale or chard)
I tablespoon olive oil
1 garlic clove, crushed
A small chunk of *grana* (grating
   cheese) such as a good
   Parmesan, *pecorino romano*, or an
   aged *asiago*
Country-style bread, preferably
   1 day old
More garlic cloves, 1 for each slice
   of bread
Tuscan olive oil

Soak the navy beans in water to cover overnight. Drain the beans, and place them in a large pot with the prosciutto or ham bone, bay leaf, garlic, onion, tomatoes, and their juice. Add water to cover. Bring to a boil, cover, and reduce heat and simmer until tender, about 2 hours. Add salt and pepper. Then stir in the oregano and parsley. Let cool to tepid.

Wash the greens well. Remove any tough stems and chop very roughly. Heat the olive oil in a heavy skillet; add the crushed garlic clove. As soon as the garlic turns golden, remove it and throw the greens into the skillet. Cover and steam for 15 to 20 minutes, stirring once or twice. Add salt and pepper. Let cool to tepid.

To make the *fettunta*, cut the bread into ¾-inch slices, then grill or toast and while still warm, rub each slice with the cut edge of a garlic clove. Set on a plate and pour virgin olive oil over. Top with the greens, then ladle some of the white bean stew over this. Grind black pepper over and add some freshly grated cheese.

Note: The beans and the greens can be prepared ahead.

(First published in the *San Francisco Chronicle*. Used by permission.)

Garlic and Parsley: Antidote or Anecdote?

≈ LYNDA BROWN ≈

IT IS COMMON "knowledge" that once you've ingested garlic, the odor on your breath can be mitigated by chewing a variety of aromatic things: coffee beans, mints, cardamom, and of course, parsley. The official position of LSR has always been that even the strongest breath "fresheners" (and what could be more fresh than fresh garlic breath?) only partially mask the odor of garlic, so why even try to eliminate the pleasant after-glow of a garlic-rich meal? Our position has recently been challenged. As we go to press, Dick Graff, a wine maker and the chairman of the board of the American Institute of Wine and Food, tells us that according to his knowledge of sulphur compounds in the wine-making process, only one thing can possibly work as an antidote to garlic breath: gargling with hydrogen peroxide. No comment.

The debate rages on: Can anything mask the odor of garlic? Lynda Brown, in a paper delivered to the Oxford Symposium in 1985—entitled "Cooks' Lore: True or False?"—offers the most definitive statement yet on the subject of parsley and garlic. Following is a major excerpt from that paper.

THE ASSOCIATION of parsley with garlic needs no introduction. Widespread throughout both Old and New World cuisines, it's as happy and successful a combination as you are likely to find. The issue under scrutiny is whether, as is often reported in herbals and general cookery books or articles, chewing parsley takes away the undeniable stink of garlic and, if so, whether there is any scientific validation for this. In other words, true or false?

As my own experience of the purported remedy has sadly always proved negative, I began my enquiry by making as thorough a search of whatever books I could lay my hands on, and by contacting those I thought likely to be more knowledgeable than I. The following is a selection of replies I received and the sort of statements one can expect:

> The best antidote to garlic breath is raw parsley. Chewing two or three sprigs of parsley will help considerably. (M. Schulman, *Garlic Cookery*)

> [Parsley] is effective as a breath sweetener when garlic or raw onions have been on the menu. (F. Shinagel, S. Rosenthal, *How Cooking Works*)

There are many ideas on how to remove the odour of garlic from the breath . . . [e.g.,] chew a coffee bean or sprig of parsley after eating. All help, I have found, but true garlic lovers know that nothing but time will completely eradicate the odour. (M. Mawso, *Herb and Spice Cookery*)

There is a very funny thing about parsley—if you chop up some of its leaves with garlic, the garlic will hardly smell at all. So if you have a fancy to eat raw or cooked onions with your meals, before you go to the dance-hall, chew a leaf or two of Parsley, and hey presto, your breath then becomes like new-mown hay. (Mrs. Grieve, broadcast, circa 1930, *Herbal Review*, summer 1981)

We are very sorry but we do not know how the association of garlic and parsley first originated, and therefore cannot help you in this instance. (The School of Herbal Medicine)

With reference to the parsley/garlic query, Mr. Cooper advises that he himself does not believe the theory that parsley takes the smell of garlic away from the breath. (The Herb Society)

The Romans used parsley to dispel the fumes of wine and Gerard writes of its power to overcome strong smells. It was probably used also by the ancient Greeks. Like many of its family— the umbellifers—it is also a useful digestive and for "expelling the wind", thus removing the gases generated by garlic and other members of the onion family. I have never found any suggestion of *how much* one should eat . . . but I have the feeling that as more intelligent research is carried out, scientific evidence may confirm many old wives' tales as having a useful thread of truth, even if they were arrived at by muddled conclusions! (Madge Hooper, Stoke Lacy Herb Garden, Bromyard)

The only [thing] you may not already know about parsley [is]: . . . Chewing parsley does neutralise the odour of onion or garlic on the breath. (Glyn Christian, *The Delicatessen Food Handbook*)

As I was conducting my inquiries, a few things struck me as being relevant. As my brief selection of quotations shows, the purported effect is by no means universally claimed. I estimated that about 40 percent of the books I consulted mentioned the association, and with varying degrees of enthusiasm.

As far as I could determine, the association—in literature at least—seems to be fairly modern. Certainly the early well-known herbals and gardening/cookbooks such as those of Turner, Culpeper, Evelyn, Gerard, Richard Bradley, etc., many of whom spoke in florid terms of garlic's stinkingness, offer no respite of parsley-sprig remedies.

The earliest mention I have found to date is in Henry Phillips' *History of Vegetables* (1821), which states, "It [parsley] should always be brought to the table when any dish is introduced that is strongly seasoned with onions, as it takes off the smell and prevents the after-taste of that strong root." I think we can fairly assume that he includes garlic in his onion tribe. Indeed, I wonder whether it might not even be Mrs. Grieve herself who is responsible for the currently popular perceived efficacy of parsley on garlic? In *A Modern Herbal* (1931) she writes: "Though the medicinal virtues of Parsley are still fully re-cognised, in former times it was considered a remedy for more disorders than it is now used for. Its imagined quality of destroying poison, to which Gerard refers, was probably attributed to the plant from its remarkable power of overcoming strong scents, even the odour of garlic being rendered almost im-perceptible when mingled with that of parsley."

The nearest I have come to finding a rational explanation so far lies in parsley's ability to act as de-odouriser due to its stated high chlorophyll content. Chlorophyll tablets are still sold as a herbal remedy for sweetening the breath and were once very popular.

> But when at last chorophyll came in I was instantly won over. What a boon and blessing to dips! What an over-riding sense of relief! Many a breach was healed that day between man and man. Even Polk-Mowbray in the end allowed the salad bowl to be lightly rubbed with a couple of heads before serving. And I don't know whether you noticed the rather respectable little ra-gout we have just been eating? Not bad for the Bluc, is it? But fear nothing. In my pocket lies a phial full of those little grey tablets which make human intercourse a rational, easy, unbut-toned sort of thing again. No more shrinking from pursed lips in the Office. We can hold our heads high once more! Let's drink a final little toast to the goddess of the F.O. shall we? I give you Chlorophyll! ("If Garlic Be the Food of Love", from *Stiff Upper Lip*, Lawrence Durrell, 1959, quoted in *The Book of Garlic*, Lloyd J. Harris)

The idea generally mooted used to be that bits of garlic get stuck in the teeth, causing the smell, which is swiftly counteracted by the de-odourising effect of parsley. This is at best an over-simplification of the way garlic works. The active principles in garlic are sulphur compounds, identified as diallyl di-sulphide (which causes the smell) and allyl thiosulphinate (responsible for gar-lic's medicinal effects and anti-bacterial activity). Both are formed as a result of the breakdown and subsequent oxidation of the parent compound, alliin, brought about by an enzyme, allinase. The alliin and allinase are separated from each other by cellular membranes. Crushing the cloves brings them into contact and sets off the reaction.

Once in the digestive system, the sulphurous compounds permeate through the blood and tissues and into the lungs, which is why garlic fed di-rectly into the stomach or alimentary canal (the things they do in the name of science) still comes through as garlicky breath. Cooking destroys the enzyme and hence reduces the effect considerably. All of which leads to that self-appointed worshipper of garlic, Lloyd J. Harris (of Lovers of the Stinking Rose, *Garlic Times*, and *The Book of Garlic* fame) to conclude that "although various antidotes for garlic odour will perhaps mask some of the odour, there is little one can do to completely eliminate the sulphurous eruptions that accompany a proper garlic repast." And one could argue that if anyone should know, he should.

With respect to parsley, there is a further flaw in the argument. Why should parsley contain any more chlorophyll than other green things? The answer is "No reason," a fact confirmed by Dr. Allen of the Botany Department of Leeds University, and Prof. Stearn, one of the leading authorities on garlic in this country [England]. As far as the chlorophyll argument is concerned, you might just as well chew on spinach, lettuce, or anything else that takes your fancy. Professor Stearn, by the way, knows of no scientific evidence to support the theory that parsley takes away the smell of garlic. Furthermore, he doesn't believe it does. As both Dr. Allen and Prof. Stearn reminded me:

> That stinking goat on yonder hill
> Feeds all day on chlorophyll.

And there, I think, we must let the matter rest.

There is, however, one more line of enquiry which might throw some light on the matter. People's reaction and ability to digest garlic varies enormously. In homeopathy, this is translated into an individual's need for garlic, or rather for the sulphurous and other compounds found within its innocent snow-white cloves, for garlic is a mine of minerals. Once a balance has been reached and your body's complex chemical needs have been satisfied, you won't smell of garlic anymore. I have yet to be brave enough to put this to the test, but remember Ford Madox Ford's beautiful mannequin? Ah, if only . . .

Similarly, therefore, it is the amount of parsley which is significant. Eat enough, so the theory goes, and you will indeed get the desired alleviation. Which might mean that I, for example, am not eating enough and which might explain why some people find parsley more beneficial as an antidote to garlic than others. There might be, after all, a human dimension as well as a scientific. I am, however, certain that glib phrases of the "one might wish to provide one's guests with a sprig of parsley" type serve no useful purpose. Although "chew great bowlfuls of the stuff" might be nearer the mark, it doesn't make as good copy, does it?

Garlic

Russian penicillin—that was the magic
of garlic, a party and cure. Sure,
you'll wrestle the flowers for fixings,
tap roots and saw branch for the ooze
of health, but you'll never get better.
I say you're living a life of leisure,
if life is life and leisure leisure.
The heart's half a prophet; it hurts
with the crabapple floating on top,
it aches just to know of the ocean—
the Old Country split off from the New—
and the acts of scissors inside you.
The heart of the East European,
poor boiler, is always born broken.
The sore heart weighs too much
for its own good. And Jewish health
is like snow in March, sometimes April.
The brothers who took their medicine
with you (garlic!) are dead now too.
The herb that beat back fever and sore
went home to its family: the lilies.

Marvin Bell
from *Residue of Song*
(Atheneum)

IV

GARLIC

The Medicine

So why has the U.S. medical establishment shown such a low level of interest in medicinal uses of garlic? The answer is probably an economic one. The costs of establishing the efficacy and safety of any new pharmaceutical are quite high. Yet, there is little profit to be made in marketing a folk remedy that people can obtain cheaply and administer to themselves.

Ross S. Feldberg, Ph.D.
Associate Professor of Biology
Tufts University

OVER THE last 10 years, there has been increasing evidence that consumption of garlic, especially fresh garlic, can prove beneficial for a variety of ailments. Most striking, I think, have been reports of garlic's effects on lowering blood cholesterol and preventing clotting in the blood. Since Dorothy Foster Sly wrote the following article, several key studies have been published, among them a report in the March 1985 Scientific American. *In that report, Dr. Eric Block of the University of Missouri reported that the medical folklore of garlic seems "to be gaining some credence." Dr. Block's research, beginning in 1971, isolates an antithrombotic agent he calls ajoene (in honor of the Spanish word for garlic, ajo), which is a derivative of allicin, a component of garlic.*

Although not yet willing to conclude that garlic has a future as a pharmaceutical drug (most researchers will not go that far until their evidence is verified by many more studies), Dr. Block did say that "experiments have since indicated that as an antithromboitic agent, ajoene is at least as potent as aspirin." He also asserts that "for now, the beneficial effects attributed to garlic are best obtained from fresh garlic."

Today in class we learned that garlic can give you vitamins and minerals. It unclogs your nose. Siberian citizens used it for money. Eleanor Roosevelt put chocolate covered garlic [sic] and she used it for her memory. It kills mosquitoes and flies. It keeps yourself warm. Dogs also like it. It helps infections.

George Boyk, 5th Grade
Mt. Prospect, IL

While doing field work with the Huichol Indians of northern Mexico, I was stung by a scorpion, which is frequently fatal. Needless to say, I was quite concerned, but an Indian simply took 2 large cloves of garlic, split them in two and bound them to the wound, the cut faces against the skin. I was then told to drink a liter or two of water and go to bed. I did, slept 10–12 hours and woke up feeling fine.

Peter Furst
Albany, NY

Further evidence of garlic's entry into modern medical and nutrition circles is readily visible. Dr. William Castelli, the man behind the Framingham Study on cholesterol, includes garlic on his list of foods that contribute to the prevention of heart disease. Also notable was the recent endorsement of garlic's health potential by Jane Brody, nutrition editor of The New York Times.

It seems as if almost every day there is a new study on garlic mentioned in the media.* I've given up trying to keep up with it all. What's encouraging for those who believe in garlic's healing benefits is that more and more of the studies mentioned in the press are by American researchers. The American medical establishment will not endorse garlic's benefits until American studies validate claims made by foreign researchers.

I think you will see from the following chapter that general acknowledgment of garlic's value among American health practitioners is just around the corner.

* As we go to press, we noted in the San Francisco Chronicle *an article on new American research that appears to confirm previous reports from Europe and Asia that garlic can control the growth of cancerous tumors.*

Out of the Pan and Into the Poultice
≈ DOROTHY FOSTER SLY ≈

Let a clove of garlic remain in her womb until dawn. If the smell is present in her mouth, then she will conceive; if not, she will not conceive.

Egyptian Papyrus Kahun
(16th century B.C.*)*

Since garlic hath powers to save from death
Bear with it though it makes unsavory breath.

Salerno Regimen of Health
(12th century A.D.*)*

WHETHER FOR predicting life or preventing death, garlic's magical-medicinal properties have long enjoyed world renown. In modern medicine, "natural" and herbal therapies are disdained and discounted, but this herb's 5000-year success as a popular therapeutic cannot be ignored. Indeed, as scientists today probe the mysteries of garlic's curative powers, *Allium sativum* is seen to withstand the tests of time. While its use as a medicine is still certainly controversial, there is now a proven scientific basis for some of garlic's best-known medicinal qualities.

Since the beginning of recorded time, garlic has figured prominently in the documents of healers. The Egyptians, the first known people to practice medicine, used the herb in tests of female fertility and as an essential ingredient in a variety of pharmaceutical preparations. The Codex Ebers papyrus, a comprehensive medical treatise dating to about 1550 B.C., logged garlic in 22 formulas for treating everything from headaches to heart problems and tumors.

Hippocrates, the Father of Medicine, in 460 B.C. recommended garlic for wounds, infections, and intestinal disorders. Fellow Greek countryman Dioscorides, a physician of the first century A.D., also encouraged the herb's use. His two master works, *Materia Medica* and *Household Remedies*, set healing standards for centuries to come; garlic figured largely in his prophylactic formulas.

Roman soldiers, meanwhile, are said to have gained athletic strength and warrior courage from their garlic-redolent diet. Roman naturalist Pliny the Elder advocated garlic remedies for some 60 ills—including diarrhea, coughs and colds, blood cleansing, and infection—vaulting the herb to glory. In 200 A.D., Galen, a Roman physician, bestowed upon garlic the nickname "Theriaca Rusticoriam"—the rustics' or people's Heal-All.

Though herbal medicines fell from favor at the close of the Middle Ages, and *Allium sativum* made little history for hundreds of years, its nickname stuck. By the sixteenth century, the English (though taking pains to keep it from their plate and palate) adopted the notion of garlic's healing value and its name became the "Poor Man's Treacle," treacle being an "uptown" preparation for whatever ails you.

The French took a more vigorous interest in garlic's curative qualities; at least among the lower classes it was de rigueur in the sixteenth century to dangle a pouch of garlic from a string around the neck. Besides repelling vampires, the garlic pendant was said to protect the wearer from falling victim to the plague.

French priests (the necklace perhaps being ill-suited to their attire) went one step further. They ate garlic—lots of it. Consequently, or so the story goes, when tending the plague-fevered and ailing, French priests remained immune to the disease, while the abstemious English priests performing the same ministrations took ill.

But the herb wasn't partial to French do-gooders, its protective powers worked just as well for ne'er-do-wells. Four thieves who plundered the dead during the Marseilles plague of 1721 claimed it was their fine swill of aged wine with garlic (better known today as garlic wine vinegar) that provided them complete immunity. While the thieves' ultimate fate is unknown, their short-term "proof" of garlic's powers heightened the herb's status in the herbals of the era. As one seventeenth-century European writer put it " . . . our Doctor [is] a good clove of Garlic."

Garlic was similarly revered in other parts of the world. The histories of India, China, Spain, and Russia, and the herbals of the American Indians, show garlic advised for ills as various as intestinal disorders and high blood pressure.

Today's herbalists recommend garlic for many of the same reasons that the ancients did—but evidence of garlic's true medicinal worth has only been recently produced. Its noteworthy success as a battlefield antiseptic during World Wars I and II is credited with triggering the interest of laboratory scientists.

In the 1940s, chemists traced the bactericidal power of *Allium sativum* to "allicin," one of the odiferous sulphur-containing compounds found in the crushed cloves. Since then, researchers in China, Hungary, Russia, and even the United States, have tested the herb's potency against a host of disease-causing bacteria and fungi.

One medical journal from China recently reported that garlic "shows promise" as a therapy for a frequently fatal form of meningitis (an inflammation of tissues surrounding the brain). Another Chinese study revealed that application of fresh slices of garlic can successfully treat infections of the inner ear.

In Hungary, garlic facials are a popular tonic for skin problems. Garlic-based pharmaceutical creams are marketed for the treatment of acne and a plethora of bacterial and fungal infections.

Allicin-containing preparations are so frequently used in Russia that the compound's been dubbed the "Russian penicillin". Neither are the anti-bacterial attributes of garlic-in-the-raw overlooked. During flu epidemics, the Soviet government is said to have imported as much as 500 tons of the herb as medicine for the masses.

Studies by botanists and microbiologists in the U.S. have corroborated some of the international findings. At the Medical College of Virginia, the studies of Dr. R. A. Fromtling show water-based (aqueous) extracts of garlic inhibit growth of *Cryptococcus neoformans*, a fungi that occurs throughout the world and causes one form of diffuse meningitis.

Similarly, Dr. Michael Tansey of the University of Indiana reports that aqueous extracts of garlic can check the growth of several species of medically important fungi and molds. Among the more notable and familiar fungi are *Candida albicans*, the cause of vaginal yeast infections; *Histoplasma capsulatum*, a dust-carried fungus that infects the respiratory tract; and dermatophytes, which causes athlete's foot and other ringworm-type skin infections.

But Tansey is not ready to prescribe garlic footbaths for jocks and joggers, nor any other kind of garlic self-treatment of infections. "I'm a botanist," says Tansey. "My research doesn't show how or if garlic would work in the human system—and that needs to be done before garlic can be used as a medicine."

Outside of bacteriology, in fact, some of the most provocative garlic research done in the last 10 years has involved human and animal subjects. A number of investigators from India, Bulgaria, Libya, and Japan, and a select few from the U.S., have shown that the herb may be a valuable palliative for such twentieth-century maladies as heart disease, diabetes, and heavy-metal poisoning.

Garlic's role in warding off heart disease is linked to its apparent ability to lower blood levels of cholesterol, a notion closely investigated by Dr. David Kritchevsky, associate director of the Wistar Institute in Philadelphia.

"I was doing postdoctoral work in Switzerland," says Kritchevsky, "when I discovered that my landlady—a 66-year-old woman who looked 44 and acted 22—attributed her good health to the fact that she ate a clove of garlic chopped up in her salad every night."

Upon hearing of the woman's unusual vigor, Kritchevsky's father quipped, "No wonder. The angel of death can't get near her." But the younger Kritchevsky, learning of garlic's peculiar powers from other Europeans as well, though he'd picked up the scent of a potentially spicy story. He decided to explore garlic's effect on heart disease through studies of blood cholesterol and the development of fatty deposits in the arteries of the heart.

His studies showed that rabbits fed a diet including up to 0.5% garlic oil had 10% lower blood cholesterol, and from 15% to 45% less fat in their arteries than rabbits fed the same diet without the oil. Later studies showed that garlic was similarly effective with rats.

Summing up international research on garlic and heart disease, Kritchevsky says that other papers have also reported that garlic can lower blood cholesterol. "The trouble is," he says, "the dosages required for humans seem pretty high. For instance, one researcher in India is giving people one-half to one ounce of garlic a day."

Indeed, clinical studies in India demonstrate that increased dietary consumption of the herb (an ounce of garlic is about half a head of cloves) can reduce blood-cholesterol levels in humans by as much as 17%. And members of the Jain sect who partake heartily of garlic and onions (sister herbs of the *Allium* family) have shown significantly lower blood levels of cholesterol and other fats than those who do not.

These "other" blood fats have been the focus of animal research by Dr. Myung Chi, a professor at Lincoln University in Missouri. Besides lowering cholesterol, Chi has found garlic effective in reducing the quantity of cholesterol-rich molecules, the low-density lipoproteins (LDLs), in blood. And he reports garlic capable of increasing blood concentrations of high-density lipoproteins (HDLs), molecules that move cholesterol out of the system. High levels of HDLs are associated with low risk of heart disease.

Currently Chi is investigating garlic's influence on a family of fatty acids called "prostaglandins," chemical mediators thought to be involved with high blood pressure. Results are disappointing so far: garlic seems to have "not much effect" on prostaglandin activity, says Chi.

Other researchers, including Dr. Martyn Bailey of Georgetown University in Washington, D.C., also have explored garlic's effect on blood constituents. Their studies have concentrated on the herb's ability to interfere with normal formation of blood clots.

A blood clot at the right time and place (say on the tip of your finger after a slip of the knife) can be a life saver. But a clot in an already plaque-clogged artery can precipitate a heart attack or stroke—and possibly death. The consensus seems to be that garlic (and onion) contains a chemical potent enough to inhibit untimely blood-clot formation and may, therefore, be useful in combating heart disease. How to apply this information? Opinions are divided: one researcher encourages extra consumption of the *Allium* herbs; other observe that aspirin is a simpler means to the same end.

At the U.S. Department of Agriculture's Human Nutrition Center in Beltsville, Maryland, garlic research has taken another tack. Work with animals by Drs. Mei Ling Chang and Margaret Johnson reinforces the reports of garlic's cholesterol-lowering ability and provides new evidence that the herb can reduce blood levels of fat and sugar, and increase the blood insulin level.

Other U.S. researchers had not looked for an association between garlic and insulin (the hormone that keeps blood sugar in check). Researchers from India, however, have reported in letters to the medical journal *Lancet* similar experimental findings. The letters prompted at least one British researcher to wonder if garlic should not be investigated as a potentially important adjunct to the diabetic diet.

But Chang and Johnson say they're not planning to continue their garlic studies. Says Chang, "During the experiments, even the rats' blood smelled like garlic. It just doesn't seem to me that anyone would be interested in smelling that much of garlic, no matter what we found it could do for them."

It's not an either/or choice, according to the Japanese entrepreneurs who have developed "Kyolic", an odor-free, aged extract of garlic. The Wakanuga Company of Japan, sole producers of the Kyolic capsules, keep information about their product's "natural fermentation" process close to the chest, but are not at all conservative about making claims for its wide-ranging therapeutic powers.

Why is the American medical establishment not convinced of garlic's appropriateness in the poultice as well as the pot? Puzzling over this dichotomy, Yale University professor Dr. Harold J. Morowitz has written in *Hospital Practice* that "it is characteristic of biological and biomedical research that one evaluates work in terms of knowing the investigators." Since most of the studies on garlic have been done by non-Western researchers, their findings are suspect. Doubts "create fraternities from which outsiders are excluded without regard to the character of their work," says Morowitz. With garlic's proponents recommending it for a bewildering variety of ills, it is second nature for Westerners to conclude that because all of the claims cannot be true, none of them are true.

In addition, scientists in the U.S. who have done research on garlic reveal they have had difficulty obtaining adequate funding to continue their studies. Not only is there general disbelief in herbal cures, but even if a natural product were proven effective it could not be patented in the U.S., so there is little reason for investment or interest on the part of pharmaceutical companies. And garlic growers apparently don't see themselves in the role of supporting medical studies.

It is therefore highly likely that the bulk of research work on garlic will continue to be done by scientists in the international community, rather than by those in the change-resistant West.

Leadership in this area of study may come from the World Health Organization (WHO), which is volubly committed to fostering investigation of the therapeutic properties of healing herbs—including garlic—in an effort to close the health gap between rich and poor countries. As one WHO spokesman has put it, there is no doubt that "modern medicine has a great deal still to learn from the collectors of herbs."

While there can be no dispute about garlic's culinary excellence, it is only through continued scientific study that we may one day learn whether there is incontrovertible logic in the rhyme: "A clove a day can keep the doctor away."

I only could afford to join LSR because I choose one most worthy organization to join with every 2nd paycheck. I'm ashamed to admit that "lovers" won out over ACLU.

K. Antanaitis
Detroit, MI

I am a poor man right now, but I can't resist LSR. I'll get my girlfriend to write you a check. Garlic makes the germs dance and awakens the brain. God is like garlic.

Phillip Gross
Davis, CA

As a holder of the American Express gold card and a member of Lovers of the Stinking Rose, I was most dismayed to learn that the American Express Company has taken offense at your Garlic Express Card. Ironically, our family generally enjoys the convenience of one card and the delight of the other card on the very same occasions.

I trust that all wounds and hurt feelings will be healed promptly and hope that American Express will come to see that, if anything, the Garlic Express Card enhances and complements its image. In the meantime, we are all looking forward to coming out to California someday, and you can be sure we never leave home without *both* cards.

Mrs. Samuel R. Shipley, III
Stafford, PA

GARLIC

A Miscellany

The emotional content of garlic almost equals its culinary value.

A.E. Grosser
Placitas Garlic Consortium
New Mexico

WHEN I DISCOVERED that Aries had been chosen by the great English herbalist, Culpepper, as the astrological sign for garlic, I realized that I had stumbled upon my own personal symbol. As a double or triple Aries (whatever that really means), garlic was for evermore my private and public charm. I am talking about the early 1970s when so many young people passing out of the 60s were looking for ways to refocus their scattered energies. Young would-be artists were doing outlandish things to create a sense of originality and surprise.

I was able to go further in my garlic self-analysis. My shape was becoming bulbous, I obviously smelled more and more like garlic, and I could even see parallels in my character with those of garlic: sharp when taken raw, yet subtle and "nut-like" when simmered slowly.

Soon I discovered that I was not alone. Les Blank made his obsessive, award-winning film, Garlic Is as Good as Ten Mothers, *and Charles Perry became the head of the Los Angeles chapter of LSR. A celebrated San Francisco restaurateur, Robert Charles, started an all-garlic restaurant near Lake Tahoe that became a meeting spot for serious garlic lovers. Through the years, others have stepped forward to play the grand garlic game, and more recently, garlic-centered theories—both medical and anthropological—have taken a turn toward the serious.*

The study of garlic's role in religious, magical, and kitchen culture took a step toward respectability recently at the Oxford Symposium held in 1985, and organized by the esteemed British food authority, Alan Davidson. Papers on garlic were delivered, and one of these, by Alicia Rios, dealt with the symbolic role of garlic in Spanish culture. She has, with one gesture, added herself to LSR's pantheon of garlic heavies. It is obvious that she has penetrated more deeply into garlic's mystery than anyone to date.

So there is considerable evidence that explorations into garlic are continuing outside as well as inside the culinary arena. Garlic is at once a serious and silly symbol, suggesting a cultural ambivalence towards garlic's primitive elements: odor, potency, flavor, and emotion. The material that follows traverses the garlic route, from sublime to ridiculous. Essentially nonculinary in content, there is always at the edge of this writing about garlic an assumption, almost an inside joke, that the reader is already addicted to garlic and is aware of the delicate fulcrum of garlic loyalism.

Garlic Graffiti in Truckee?

≈ L. JOHN HARRIS ≈

NEXT TO Berkeley's celebrated Chez Panisse, the restaurant most closely identified with garlic is La Vieille Maison in Truckee, California. Unconfirmed rumors have it that The Old House, as it was known during the Gold Rush, is not currently open for business. This is indeed sad, for La Vieille Maison was a sacred shrine for Lovers of the Stinking Rose.

In about 1976, I heard that a garlic theme restaurant had just opened near Lake Tahoe. I rushed up to the Sierras and discovered a charming bistro and delicious, garlicky cuisine served by famed restaurateur Robert Charles and his wife Amora. Everything on the menu had fresh garlic in it, and instead of butter, aïoli was served with the bread.

For years, I would go every winter to Truckee by train. It was a romantic, almost religious pilgrimage: a 5-hour train ride through breathtaking Sierra scenery, a short walk to a rustic boarding house where I would drop off my bags, another short walk to La Vieille Maison for a garlic-laden meal, and then back

The Certificate of a Bona Fide Garlic Peeler was handed out to repeat customers at La Vieille Maison restaurant in Truckee, California. Restaurateur Robert Charles made garlic the theme of his restaurant.

to a blissful slumber. Those were precious days, and Robert was always a gen-
erous and delightful patron.

A trademark of Robert Charles' restaurants (and he had many hit restaurants in San Francisco before moving to Truckee) is the graffiti on the walls.
His garlic bistro in Truckee had walls covered with garlic graffiti. One year I
went with the intention of recording the graffiti. I discovered that the first few
years' worth was no longer visible, due to changes at the restaurant. But I did
manage to record the newer scrawls, dating from 1980.

Garlic is the cynic's aphrodisiac!

> *Raiders of the lost garlic*
> *Cathryn Kahn, 8/20/81*

Un repas sans l'ail . . .
I'd rather die.

> *D.L. '81*

History repeats itself, as does garlic.

> *Anon.*

The only thing better than garlic for dinner is getting married
for lunch.

> *Steve and Kaye*

We ate here on vacation in July.
We ate so much garlic I thought we'd die.
The friends were great, the food the same,
I only have the garlic to blame.

> *Anon.*

Sex and garlic, garlic and sex,
If we keep this up, we'll both be wrecks.

> *J. the fox and friend, 2/4/82*

For a real garlic massage, ask for George.

> *Anon.*

There once was a fine fellow
Who found Truckee very mellow
He came from Marin
With a little chagrin
And discovered garlic jello!

> *Anon.*

Here's to life, love, & the pursuit of garlic.
F. & B.

Garlic makes gourmands out of gourmets.
Gay & Frank, 5/25/80

Pot—Drug of the 60s
Coke—Drug of the 70s
Garlic—Drug of the 80s

Mark Evans

If we had a garlic farmer for President, we'd have a much better
stink in Congress.
Alan Tarel, 7/24/80

You only go around once in life—go for the gusto and the garlic.
Leilanie et al., 6/13/81

Peachy Nietzsche and garlic gamut
After this, all other restaurants Kaput!.
LMH, 3/81

Garlic is hardcore.
Gertie & Karen

Eat your heart out Dracula!
MJH, 4/17/81

A clove a day keeps MacDonalds at bay!
Anon.

Here is to La Vieille Maison, where garlic is like good sex—it
comes up again and again, and again.
Earle & Jeanne, 10/31/80

Although La Vieille Maison may no longer be operating, you can catch
glimpses of it in two films: *Garlic Is as Good as Ten Mothers* by Les Blank has
some scenes filmed at the restaurant, and another film called *Garlic, The Spice
of Life*, part of a television series made in England on spices of the world, is now
available on video cassette. The latter film is shot entirely at La Vieille Maison,
and it features a crazy LSR dinner, complete with silliness and garlic repartee
by Charles Perry, myself, and other LSR members. If you can't find the video,
a transcription of the film is available in the book, *The Spice of Life* by Sheldon
Greenberg and Elizabeth Lambert Ortiz (The Amaryllis Press).

The Best of Charles Perry, Fearless Garlic Writer

IN The Book of Garlic, *there is a section of writings by Charles McCabe, "The Fearless Spectator" in the* San Francisco Chronicle. *Mr. McCabe had written frequently about garlic before it had become chic, and we dubbed him the Fearless Garlic Eater. Mr. McCabe passed away a few years back, and had he lived longer, I'm sure we would have included more of his garlic mots here. We are lucky, however, that Mr. McCabe was not the only fearless garlic eater or writer. Another Charles has been putting ink to garlic skins for a long while, and LSR has been fortunate to have Mr. Perry's work in* Garlic Times.

Charles Perry's brilliance as a writer and scholar is surpassed only by his zaniness, or in garlic terms, his sweet nuttiness. In another, less cuisine-conscious era, he would qualify as an egg head. Bulb head is more appropriate now.

Perhaps Charley has, more than anyone, brought intelligence, wit and true gastronomic savvy to the Garlic Revolution. Sitting with Charley at a Chez Panisse Garlic Festival, playing around with euphemisms for the word Vampire, is a pleasure few garlic lovers have had the opportunity to experience. The world of garlic lovers owes Charley much, and for those who have not had the pleasure of meeting him, we hope this collection of his garlic writings excerpted from Garlic Times *will suffice.*

Vampire Interests Dictate to New West

IN 1980, California Magazine *(then* New West*) published an article that angered Charles Perry. Here is his reply as published in* Garlic Times.

New West has extended its pages to a carefully timed propaganda attack commissioned by the bloodsuckers. Colman Andrews' viciously titled "Everything But the Kitchen Stink" (*New West*, May 19, p. 88), under false progressive colors, does the work of Andrews' day-sleeping bosses using a congeries of gross errors, slippery evasions and base lies, only a few of which can be exposed here.

1. Andrews twists an exploratory attempt to establish dialogue into a "threat" from a mysterious "goon". What was threatened.¿

2. He twists words like a true jingo and calls garlic defenders "botanical racists". The fact is that chives, leeks, etc., although good comradely vegetables, have never been subject to the cruel and *clearly organized* campaign of repression that garlic has. Also, none of the milder alliums is the slightest against Andrews' pals, who don't sit down to eat. Coincidence¿

Charles Perry, Southern California leader of Lovers of the Stinking Rose, was called a "garlic goon" by *New West* magazine (now *California* magazine). Charley has been fighting back ever since.

3. In his only attempt to face the central, political issue of garlic, Andrews tells his biggest "big lie": that England, a garlic-deprived country, does not suffer from vampires. THE TRUTH IS THE EXACT REVERSE! England is a textbook example of what can happen to a democratic country when vampiricism is unchecked! The official English line that there are no vampires, the open anti-garlicist position of its ruling classes, and the well-known dreariness of English life—tea, birdwatching, vicars, halting conversations, terrible food, and endemic upper-lip disorders—are but three aspects of a single specter: the oft-noted but rarely analyzed "bloodlessness" of a nation deprived of the means of self-defense.

4. Right-metabolizing people—people who can eat solid food, if you take our meaning—have no objection to sincere garlic extremism such as is documented in *Garlic Is as Good as Ten Mothers*. We believe it is no coincidence that Andrews' hatchet-job was commissioned by his hairy-palmed bosses to precede the recent Los Angeles opening of this explosive film.

Wake up, America! You know who these "people" are, and the serum they want isn't truth serum! The blood is starting to hit the fan! It's time to *take up the bulb* and *breathe tall!*

Greek Garlic

Garlic, as we know, is native to western Asia. It is generally assumed that the Greeks learned about it from some people of Asia minor, such as the Phrygians.

But hold on. Nobody knows where the Greek word for garlic (*skordon*, or as it usually appears with the definite article, *to skordon*) originated. Curiously, the Berber peoples of North Africa have a word for garlic that is similar to *to skordon*. It is basically *tiskert* (Tuareg *taskert*, Rif *zaskhers*, etc.).

Now, did the Berbers learn of garlic from the Greeks, assuming that *to skordon* was one word? Or did the Greeks learn about garlic during the Mycenean or Cretan period in their trading with Egypt, where outside the Nile Valley the people spoke Berber languages?

Or is it back to Atlantis?

A Vampire is A Vampire Is A . . .

Here's a collection of slang expressions for "Vampire" that came out of conversations at the Chez Panisse Garlic Festival and a long, hallucinatory drive to L.A. on Route 5!

a red-blooded American, once removed

a coffin snoozer

a hemo

stakebait

an all-night diner

a garlic chicken

a 98.6 chowder hound

one of your web-fingered connoisseurs

a clotlicker

dribblefangs (dribble-dentures)

a day sleeper

a plasma rustler

a throat fetishist

Chief Big Hickey

slobberchops (messy eater, slurper)

a fan of that special beet juice

old pink-toothbrush

a paleface (has a deep moontan)

a bloodjacker

a liquid-diet fatty

Phrases: "a cheap date—dinner's always on you," "bites but doesn't chew," "eats and flies," "the crimson popsicle—trouble tonight but a puddle in the morning" ("a noon melter").

Historical English Garlic Aversion Updated

On September 19th and 20th, I was in England delivering a paper on three medieval Arabic cookbooks at a symposium at Oxford. One of the interesting papers delivered was by Prof. Jean-Louis Flandrin, who has been doing a statistical analysis of the ingredients called for in cookbooks ranging from Apicius (2nd to 4th centuries A.D.) to the 18th century. He found that it was in the 17th century that the French discovered an aversion to "spicy" food (i.e., food flavored with any spice but pepper, clove, or nutmeg) and mint. And it was in the same century that the English realized how awful garlic was. Before that time, he pointed out, there were English proverbs about garlic like those in other countries, showing "a certain affection" for the bulb and accepting the strong smell as a natural part of life. "The mortar always stinks of the garlic," etc. Not a lusty appetite for it, but an intimacy. But in the 17th century the old proverb, "He could eat my heart without salt" (meaning he harbors a bitter animosity toward me, he could kill me), starts to appear in the form, "He could eat my heart with garlic"—meaning that garlic was now a deterrent to eating.

Is it a result of the accession of the Stuarts? The founding of the East India Company? The threat of Spanish expansionism in The Netherlands and elsewhere? My personal suspicion is that it was an invasion of vampires from the Brahmin caste of India—the English always liked to deal with the upper crust, and perhaps some plague ship of mantra-mutterers named things like Nosferatuswami arrived in London. England, being an island, had perhaps no native vampires and was thus as vulnerable as Plains Indians were to smallpox.

Garlic Pride

THIS PRONOUNCEMENT was handed out by Charles and his merry band of garlic nuts at the annual Pasadena Doo-Dah parade (held in September), a spoof of the New Year's day Rose Bowl parade. Charley and gang make a garlic float every year and push it along, throwing garlic cloves to and at the crowds.

Yes, we are proud garlicpersons who have Come Out of the Back Porch, breathing tall and free! We're no longer afraid to speak out against the repressive coffinbreath establishment that has terrorized generations with sneers and oppressive innuendo! We're through apologizing! We're through begging for tolerance! We're going on the offensive! We demand to be represented in cookbooks, etiquette columns, and the workplace as positive, fragrant role models! We demand right-to-breath!

We're speaking out, telling it like it is, naming species! We don't mince words about whom we're up against—figure it out for yourself. *Who* benefits from prejudice against garlic? *Who* has a vested interest in banishing this Holy Bulb, healthful condiment, and comforter of all right-metabolizing human beings? A bat-winged pack of hairy-palmed fly-by-nights, that's who! A blood-sucking rabble of Transylvanian transfusionites! A flapping block of Midnight Gourmets who fatten on our precious oxygen-bearing fluids and try to dictate what we can put on our salads in the bargain! Those pasty-faced, cape-waving Hemogoblins who don't exactly sit down to dine! Those liquid-diet connoisseurs who go for that "special beet juice"! Those skulking, squeaking day-sleepers who bat-nap in the kind of bed that has a *lid* on it, if you catch our drift! In a word, that whole dribble-fanged stakebait crowd that a wiser age would have exposed to the light of day and then swept up and fed to the rutabagas!

The Red Fluid is hitting the fan! It's time to Bite the Bulb! Do you want to have to check your windows every night for fear of waking up with the Big Hickey? Do you want to see America turned into a doormat for the Patent Leather Jackboot of these tuxedoed gourmets whose fussy sense of smell is revolted by Friendly Mr. Garlic but who can't exactly be said to have fastidious table manners? Do you want to watch a bunch of Hemos run riot, undermining the capillary system and drinking a lot of blood that doesn't belong to them?

Then join us! Breathe Proud, Breathe Tall, Breathe Free! Celebrate with us the Innocence of Garlic with our Garlic Princess and Symbolic Dancing Garlic Heads! Reek havoc on the Batboys and their dupes and running dogs! Don't go out after dark without a loaded garlic press! Always order the Italian salad dressing! Combat blandbreath!

At the turn of the century, these Arleux citizens posed with their favorite local product. One can imagine this scene at the turn of any century, as far back as garlic has been grown.

A Contemporary Garlic Legend: Life in the Land of the Bland

≈ JAMES PAUL ≈

WHEN THE First People gathered in tribes, they sought food all day, hunting and gathering. It was an exciting life, eating food and avoiding being food. And it had its occasional joys, like the taste of wild garlic, that power on the palate among the mild tubers and grains.

Even then people said, "Life is wild enough," and sought an easy path. One tribe among the First People turned away from garlic, and sought blander food. They grew better and better, too, at finding what they sought, and they soon grew their own grains and tamed wild animals, and they built a village wherein they could live in safety. So they came to dwell in The Land of the Bland.

They left the wild world behind, and garlic with it, and the garlic grew wild, the new moons of its cloves cool in the dark earth.

Years passed, and a weakness of spirit rose in the hearts of the people in the Land of the Bland, as if within them wild creatures were pining. The Elders of the village also felt a listlessness they could banish only by sitting in council, and speaking of the old days, when the tribe was wild and life was exciting. And though the elders would laugh in these councils, they would feel even more dispirited when they were done.

One night, as the elders told their old stories, a strange and ancient personage suddenly appeared in the meeting hall. She wore wild, colorful garments, and her hair was like the wind. And around her neck she wore the braided stems of garlic, garlic bulbs hanging heavily from them. The elders sat in surprise and silence, as some wildness wafted through the room.

"I have heard," the strange and ancient personage began, "that you gather here to pine like tame animals. Well, if you want your wildness back, you'd better ask me, for I have been its sole protector, all these years.

"For I live as you once lived, gathering my food in the forests. You are, you know, what you eat."

Among the elders was one who was very tame. He was, in fact, expert at taming others, and he said: "How dare you come here, with your insults and your wild smell? Whatever you have brought us, we have a better thing in the village."

"Do you have a better garlic?" said the strange and ancient personage, dangling a few of the bulbs on her braided necklace.

The elders laughed out loud at this absurd suggestion. She broke one of the bulbs and began peeling its cloves. The elders, quiet now, looked nervously about, and tried to grumble. "Let's see," said the S. and A. P., "who will taste this herb to see if you have a better thing here?"

No one would answer her. They were cowed. "Just as I thought," she said. "You're so tame that you're afraid of a vegetable." And she laughed in their faces, and popped one of the bare cloves into her mouth.

The Eldest of the Elders rose in his seat as she chewed the garlic. "I remember! I remember!" he shouted. "I remember the taste of garlic!" He was weeping tears of joy.

"May I have a clove of garlic, please?" he asked meekly.

Astonished, the Elders watched the Eldest eat a clove of garlic. Even as he chewed, he began to laugh. Soon the others crowded around the strange and ancient personage, each asking for and getting a clove of garlic. As they ate, the council chamber of the Elders of the Land of the Bland filled with laughter and with the wild fragrance of garlic.

And so the tribe changed its name to the Lovers of the Stinking Rose and went merrily forth, led by the strange and ancient personage and living happily ever after.

Garlic—A Kitchen Amulet

≈ ALICIA RIOS ≈

WHEN I first received a copy of Alicia Rios' essay, "Garlic—A Kitchen Amulet," I was stunned. Here was a fascinating, almost impassioned demonstration of garlic's deep, deep role in culture. From the earliest times, when foods were magic and medicine as well as nourishment, garlic has had a critical role in many cultures. In Spain, Ms. Rios' native land, this was especially true.

We have excerpted passages (with permission) from her paper, delivered at the Oxford Symposium, 1985.

Garlic the Symbol

Garlic is a magical plant used in cooking. Among the magical plants, garlic has the greatest number of culinary uses. It is our intention to establish the reasons why garlic has acquired, along the course of history, its powerful magical connotations.

In our opinion, the process by which garlic acquires symbolic connotations is based on two essential facts that explain the phenomenon and constitute the premises of this study:

1. The sensorial qualities of its strong odour and persistent flavour account for its use in cooking.

2. Healing properties, however, account for its connotations as a symbol. Garlic has been used for centuries both as healing and preventative medicine in a variety of ailments. . . . [W]e might venture to state that plants commonly used in cooking have acquired a magical appeal inasmuch as their healing properties have been tried and confirmed, and that this usefulness is what lends force to their symbolic dimension.

We believe the symbolic elements in garlic are related to the specific organoleptic qualities of odour and flavour. These are in turn inseparable from its active and healing properties. Without its flavour and odour there would be no magic, no healing, no spicing. As we will see later on, sensory functions related to flavour and odour have very peculiar resonances in human behaviour. Their significance is very specific. In approaching these complexes of questions and answers, we observe that, although highly conditioned by cultural habits, we are also confronted with the deep chasms of irrational behaviour. This is possibly due to the fact that we tread upon the ground of the most archaic levels of human behaviour, which in being the most primal, the least corticated, are nearest to the purely instinctive and unconscious motivation.

One of the reasons why garlic acquired symbolic connotations might be due to the impact its manipulation and consumption has on the psyche, i.e., the very experiencing of garlic. Physiologically, garlic stimulates the most archaic and least corticated zones of the brain, which responses are of an emotional and hedonic character. Emotion, acceptance-rejection, pleasure-displeasure are the consequences and immediate stimulus of an exposure to garlic. Irrationality is the attribute of these sensations. They trigger off deep dynamisms associated with ancestral memories and fantasies stretching along the magma of our collective unconscious. These unconscious responses are not accessible to consciousness, but do impregnate our sense of taste and smell. We believe this to be a major factor in the magical value given to garlic. . . .

Garlic as a Magical Plant

If psychological experience is interpreted as material experience, then the healer and the priest are the exorcists that liberate the vital spirits locked in nature, and under the invocation of the demonic or the divine, the life of a given subject is modified or revived. Garlic has been one of the favourite vehicles for these magical acts since earliest antiquity. In its origin, the association of odour and flavour with magical and healing properties was due to the characteristics of heat, strength, expansiveness, and volatilization found in garlic. Its smell was classified by Zwaardemaker among the putrid ones ... with rotten eggs, arsenic-hydrogen, chlorine, and bromine. Linnaeus classifies its flavour as acrid.... The magic found in the vegetable kingdom lies in the knowledge of the plants' spirit. What spirits dwell in garlic? Where do its magical powers come from? Which is its animus? Under what sign comes its manna?

Garlic, Sulphur and Fire

Garlic is volatile and hot. It expresses sulphur and fire. Sulphur and sulphuric acid held an interest to the alchemists as a special substance capable of materializing the volatile. Paracelsus groups it astrologically under the sign of Aries. It comprises the three basic substances necessary for all bodies: sulphur signified fire, water signified mercury, and salt signified the earth .... Raimon Llull says, in *The Tree of Marvels*, "My son, God has given man his sense of smell to smell out the evil vapours, so he will fear suffering the vapours of hell, sulphur and many foul smelling things; because in hell all the bodies of men shall stink and their breath shall stink, and their limbs shall stink, according to the sins committed in this world with those very limbs .... "

Littré mentions that the Hippocratic school recommended applying foul smelling substances in the nostrils to counteract attacks of hysteria, which shows the existence of a therapy based on the apotropaic power of foul smelling substances such as sulphur, well known for driving demons away .... Garlic contained the necessary *dynamis* for expelling spirits.

Odour and Mysticism

Bad smell is associated with evil, the devil, and sin. But just as it is the symbol of evil, it in turn serves to drive evil away, to cast it out. Once again it is usefulness that confirms the value of the symbol. Along the course of social and religious history, scents and odours of all kinds have found a place in the most important mystical ceremonies.

Garlic had a function as an ointment against psychic attack, turning hidden forces into man's allies. But as mankind developed its esthetic sense it became aware that bad smells might offend the gods. This could well be the reason for the prohibitions stated earlier. Also the acute awareness of one's own bodily odours lends weight to the rooted prejudice against garlic in Anglo-Saxon cultures, despite its proven healing properties.

In the Bible, the Book of Tobias mentions the utility of bad odour. And the book of Spanish sayings reads: "Garlic and pure wine and then you will know who each one is." Sulphur, vestige of the smell of allium, is used to sober up drunkards, its fumes make the fainted come to, and shop windows are sprinkled with its powder to keep dogs away. The dog is a symbol of death, Cerberus the doorkeeper, and yet it flees at the first whiff of sulphur.

Conclusion

From the earliest times the most basic ingredients we use in our cooking have been imbued with magical and symbolic significance. This significance has been lost inasmuch as we have lost the religious sense of life and death, sickness and health, that explained all phenomena as the spiritual and physical emanations of the god-head. There can be no conception of magic without some intimation of divinity. To the religious mind, life itself is magic: its myriad souls and creatures and our daily food stemming from a great act of creation.

... In my opinion the cook is a veritable exorcist, for in combating garlic with its own sign, fire, he quells its pungent demon to transform the most insipid dishes into a tasty and delectable meal.

Joining the Garlic Revolution

YOU ARE A LOVER of the stinking rose, and, if after reading this book you are so jazzed up about garlic that becoming a member of Lovers of the Stinking Rose is the logical thing to do, of course, you can join LSR!

But take note: our goal is not to simply solicit members, but rather to celebrate garlic and help others to celebrate. So we suggest that you:

≈ *Start your own chapter of LSR in your community.*

≈ *Find a movie theater to show Les Blank's* Garlic Is as Good as Ten Mothers.

≈ *Encourage local restaurants to sponsor garlic dinners.*

As you can see, we're suggesting that you create your own garlic festival. We can help you to do this—and it's not hard.

It would also be helpful if you filled out the questionnaire that appears in The Book of Garlic. *Your answers will allow us to assess the changes in garlic consumption as the years go by. And by sending us your recipes, jokes, poems, letters, and so forth, we can continue our beloved task of gathering the materials for a future collection of garlic expressions.*

How To Join LSR

IF YOU WANT to make it official, you can join LSR and receive a two-year subscription to the Garlic Times *newsletter, and discounts on "mail odor" items such as garlic presses, T-shirts, cookbooks, and the like.*

All new members receive, in addition to the above, a copy of The Book of Garlic. *(If you already have* The Book of Garlic, *and don't want another copy, we will substitute either another copy of* The Official Garlic Lovers Handbook *or another cookbook from our mail odor catalog that you will receive as soon as you join LSR.)*

Membership Price: $25.00 (includes book, two-year newsletter subscription, and discounts on "mail odor" items).

Gift memberships: If you are already a member, or want to join for yourself and a friend, the second membership, and all additional ones, are $16.00.

Sample issue of *Garlic Times:* Send $1.00 (please, no cash) and you will receive the latest issue of the newsletter and also complete information on LSR.

Garlic Is as Good as Ten Mothers: This film by Les Blank and Maureen Gosling is available on VHS or Beta video casettes. Members pay $45 plus $2 for shipping and handling. Non-members pay $49.95 plus $2 for shipping and handling.

Send check or money order to:
> Lovers of the Stinking Rose
> c/o Aris Books—Dept. OGLH
> 1621 Fifth Street
> Berkeley, CA 94710

Please make checks out to: Aris Books/LSR. (All prices are subject to change.)

The Book of Garlic
≈ BY LLOYD J. HARRIS ≈

288 pages, paper, $10.95

A special cloth, gift edition, signed by the author: $25.00.

The most comprehensive presentation on garlic in the world. Translated into six languages, and with over 75,000 copies sold in English, it has become the bible of garlic lovers the world over. History, folklore, medical research, jokes, and over 100 recipes, plus a wealth of culinary information on garlic.

"Highly entertaining... "

Gourmet Magazine

" ...a delightful romp of folklore, legends, comedy, historical fact and recipes."

The Des Moines Register

Garlic Times

'The *Garlic Times* newsletter is a stimulating blend of healthful fact and frolic."

Health Quarterly

"The *Garlic Times* is a wonderful publication."

The New Orleans Times-Picayune

Garlic Bibliography

SEVERAL BOOKS have been written on garlic over the last decade (mostly recipe collections). There seems, in fact, to be an acceleration of such books, as you will see from the chronological bibliography below, based on the Lovers of the Stinking Rose library.

1974 *The Book of Garlic* by Lloyd J. Harris. Panjandrum Press. San Francisco.

1974 *Garlic Therapy* by Tadashi Watanabe. Japan Publications. Tokyo.

1975 *The Great Garlic Cookbook* by Barbara Friedlander and Bob Cato. Collier Books. New York.

1975 *The Book of Garlic* by Lloyd J. Harris. Holt Rinehart & Winston. New York. (Revised, hardcover edition)

1979 *The Book of Garlic* by Lloyd J. Harris. Aris Books. Berkeley, Calif. (Third revised edition, paper)

1980 *The Garlic Lovers' Cookbook* from Gilroy. Celestial Arts. Berkeley, Calif.

1980 *Garlic, The Powerful Panacea* by Paul Simons. Thorsons Publishers Limited. Wellingborough, Northamptonshire, Great Britain.

1983 *The Little Garlic Book* by Linda Doeser and Rosamond Richardson. St. Martins. New York.

1983 *Garlic Cookery* by Martha R. Shulman. Thorsons. New York.

1984 *Garlic* by Sue Kreitzman. Harmony Books. New York.

1985 *The Garlic Lovers' Cookbook* from Gilroy. Volume II. Celestial Arts. Berkeley, Calif.

Foreign editions of *The Book of Garlic*
Garlic Book. Japan. 1978.
L'ail. Editions Guy Authier. Paris, France. 1978.
Nicht nur gegen Vampire (*Not Only for Vampires*). SV International. Zurich, Switzerland. 1981.
Nicht nur gegen Vampire. Rowohlt. Hamburg, West Germany. 1984.
(An edition in Hebrew is forthcoming.)